Saturday Night at the Open Door Cafe

by
Caron Ward

1663 Liberty Drive, Suite 200
Bloomington, Indiana 47403
(800) 839-8640
www.AuthorHouse.com

This is a work of non-fiction. Permission has been granted by the individuals whose characterizations appear herein. Other characters are composites of the many people who visited The Open Door Cafe for illustration purposes.

Open Door Cafe and **The Open Door Cafe logo** *are registered trademarks of Open Door Cafe Ministries, a not for profit organization, and may not be used in any form except with prior permission from the author.*

© 2006 Caron Ward. All Rights Reserved.

No part of this book may be reproduced, stored in a retrieval system, or transmitted by any means without the written permission of the author.

First published by AuthorHouse 12/28/2005

ISBN: 1-4208-4211-0 (sc)

Library of Congress Control Number: 2005905259

Printed in the United States of America
Bloomington, Indiana

This book is printed on acid-free paper.

For *everyone* who has ever dreamed of doing the impossible, the *remarkable*, with almost nothing at all.

Acknowledgements

With deep appreciation to my children, for their love and incredible patience with all my Big Ideas and Happy Accidents, but mostly for just being themselves. Each one, in every way, is a gift, and every one of them carries in them their own Big Idea.

I am indebted to Jeri and Ron Murray, who believed in this endeavor enough to make it a reality, and to whom I owe the ultimate success of this work. Without them, this story could never reach the very ones who need so desperately to read it.

Prologue

Sometimes, in the most ordinary of things, we find the remarkable and the miraculous.

It is hiding there — an Honest to Goodness Miracle—maybe even your miracle—right in the middle of the mundane and ridiculous, perhaps even more often in the middle of the tragic and terrible. It is often shimmering right below the surface of the Waters of Uncertainty, when our eyes are fixed on some distant point— as if our solution lay "Out There" somewhere. Perhaps we are distracted by something, such as an unmet need or an ancient longing, or our unanswered prayer, and we are looking for our miracle to come in another form or from a distant source. Our miracle always seems to lie waaaay out there on the horizon line, so far away we cannot see it. But if we were to change our perspective, slowly rising above our vantage point, and see it from above, we would see our miracle directly before us, as bright and as full of hope as any dream might be.

And on some occasions, we don't get our miracle at all. We get a different miracle.

They say that adventures can begin right in your own backyard. But, you know, I think the best ones— the most amazing ones— begin inside your heart. That is where the vast uncharted waters lie; it is where the wilderness is untamed, terrifying and mysterious, where anything can happen.

We so often we think a change of scene or a change of careers, even a change of partners, will bring what we are longing for — relief from the everyday-going-through-the-motions-of-life, relief from the burden of mistakes and regret, relief from the muggings of life, relief from those things you did not choose willingly, or perhaps chose mistakenly.

But it isn't the change of scenery that will do it for us.

No, the thing we really need is a change of heart. The catalyst for this change often comes disguised as our unmet needs. Or our private hell. This is because painful events and circumstances are often the only thing strong enough to get our attention. However, if you listen intently, holding your breath if you must, the way you listen for a strange noise in the night, you will hear something you didn't count on.

Someone is calling to us out of those longings, from the other side of your hell.

It is The Voice that whispers to you at a stoplight. It is the Voice beneath the constant cacophony of the top-forty station (even the almost-secular style of the Christian radio station); under the busy, gotta-get-it-all-while-the-gettin's-good lifestyle we subject ourselves to (and I don't mean just having it all, but also Doing It All). It is the Voice that is heard in the ear-ringing solitude of waking too early —or of going to bed too late. It is in our private yearnings and in our dark dreams. It is a Voice that sings a different song below the surface of those murky waters; and it is wooing us into the Adventure of a Lifetime— because it involves eternity. It involves bigger ideas like love for humanity, courage, and self-sacrifice, honor and perhaps even suffering.

Some of you are wincing.

Nothing less will do, after all, when it is an Epic Adventure that you wish for—the stakes must be high and you must play for keeps. To enjoy this thrill you must commit your life to an unknown, yet eternal epic.

It, the calling, your life's epic story, must be something filled with purpose and it must have eternal significance. It must not be All About You.

You must listen for it, The Voice. You must silence the little voices of vanity and futility, the voices that clamber like ill-behaved children in a restaurant for attention; for His voice is soft, and it is fleeting. He speaks to you through strings of coincidences that are woven through your life. You just might miss it while you're turning that dial, or taking up another hobby, or buying yet another toy in a fleeting effort to give your life meaning.

As the biblical account goes, after the death of Moses who led the children of Israel through the desert to the edge of the Promised Land, the story goes on. Joshua, Moses' successor, stood at the water's edge, ready to cross the Jordan to Canaan. The river was at flood stage, as it always was that time of year. He tells the leaders of the tribes of Israel to gather a large stone and at his command they were to step into the water. He reminds them of the incident at the Red Sea and instructs them to likewise take that step of faith.

The purpose of the stones? When they reached the middle of the river they were to place their stone there on dry ground as a monument to God's greatness. So there they stood, stone in hand, looking at all that water rushing past their feet and muttering. They must've thought Joshua was as crazy as a loon. But when they took that first step, as the story goes, the waters receded and they crossed on dry land. The waters were raging at flood stage until their toes touched that cold water.

Somewhere in the middle of the Jordan River, under all that water, there is a pile of twelve stones.

We have all stood on our side of a Jordan River, longing for the other side, where our Promised Land, our destiny, lies. Behind us lurks our personal little Egypt and a certain enslavement of the mind and heart.

You do remember Egypt don't you? Yeah, Egypt —the land of the Comfortable & Convenient. Where the beer was stale, but hey, it was home.

I wonder how many Christians are sitting comfortably in their pew, putting in their time, tipping God His ten percent each Sunday and feel that they've given enough? PUNCH! goes their time card in the Spiritual Time Clock. They all but brush their hands together a few times and think, "Yep! Got that done! Good for another week"

Life as usual. After all, it is about building our personal empire, isn't it? It is about leaving behind a financial legacy to our kids, isn't it? It is all about us, isn't it?

Couldn't we get more bang for the buck if we got behind some of the people who actually want to do something remarkable for others on behalf of God Himself, and leave to our kids the legacy of Making a Difference? It doesn't happen by accident, you know, but by modeling that behavior.

Imagine your life at the end of your life.

What will you realize you should have done, or could have done? What is it all about, anyway? Won't some things have been worth taking a risk?

Yet, here we stand on our River Jordan. Half-afraid to feel the cold and raging waters, we are, and yet we know-that-we-know that those same waters, so harsh and cruel and overwhelming, will be the very thing that brings our metamorphosis from what we were resigned to be, to the person we always dreamed of being. We will be transformed from what once we were, into who we were always meant to be when we summon the courage to commit ourselves to a higher purpose. Getting from who we are to who we will be will involve sacrifice of our old comfortable ways and it will mean embracing an unknown future. It will mean Change. The Voice urges us to take a step, to fling ourselves in. And it is then that we know that we must take the Promised Land with nothing more than what is at hand.

A stone. A staff. Or maybe something like, well—a teacup.

There's nothing particularly impressive in that inventory. But in the hand of The Creator of It All, and by faith in Him, they become powerful extensions from His world into ours. The very thing that God can use to restore hope to a human heart or bring down a wall may, at this very moment, be sitting right in front of you on the coffee table, or it may be out in the garage. It may be inside your jail cell. You may have thought it was all in your mind.

Of course it doesn't make sense—the smallest of tools effecting the greatest of change. But let's face it, God is full of irony and paradox. We who are finite can only partially glimpse the ever far-reaching consequences of our influence. Yet in all of this, the truly remarkable thing is not that the tools are what they are, but that there is a regular Joe who is willing to surrender every bright dream and shining self-ambition for just one shot at being God's "yes man" (or woman). Just one small foot soldier who will trade in his small dreams, his tall tale, for a true story of adventure on the high seas.

A word of caution, here, my friend. This Romance, this Adventure— is swashbuckling at it's finest— and it is not for the faint of heart. For like all great epics of love and high adventure, the cost is high. It will cost you everything, including your life. You, yourself, will change. You will look back at what you once were and you wouldn't trade what you've become for all the fleshpots of Egypt.

This is what they call the Strong Stuff.

What I am writing is a gift to you. It is a tale of walking through the fire, of losing everything, only to find — well, everything. But it is also a story of incredible blessing and intimacy. It is the story of a miracle — my very own miracle— and it touched everyone I knew. The best part, however, is that it's all true. Every word of it!

Are you ready? Cast away your self-doubt, your worry, and mostly your fear. Fear is nothing but a petty thief, and if you let him, he'll steal your very life.

But you know, I think you can take him.

Chapter 1

All was dark and still and quiet as the grave the last time I was there.

It was early in December, and while the sky that day had been so very clear and bright and blue, it was only a smudge of pink and violet between the frozen black branches by the time we pulled into the narrow driveway. Snow was still on the ground and it would snow again that night by what the weather report said.

I turned the ignition off and just sat there. I wondered to myself if it was a mistake to even come. I listened in the silence and gathered my resolve- all three shreds of it- and got out of the car, quietly pushing the door shut. His car pulled closely in behind my own

The street was undergoing intense reconstruction after several decades of neglect, and seemed more like a bombsite than a residential street in a small Midwest town. The very street was gone, as were the cobblestones below it, and workmen had dug down below that to the storm sewer and all the entrails of my two hundred year-old town.

He stood on the driver's side of his car and I had already made my way between the two cars and was standing on the passenger side across from him. I looked up at his familiar kindly face.

"Are you *sure* you want to do this?" he asked.

We stood there in the short driveway, already shivering in the darkness. He closed his car door and the echo between the houses hung in the clear cold air. Leaning forward, and with his forearms resting on the top of the car, he looked down at his enormous folded hands and then at my face. So cautious and sensible, he is the perfect blend of poet and social scientist. That's what everyone loves about Ron. He is like a friendly giant, full of a rare graciousness lost in the mayhem of life in a New York minute.

" 'Am I sure I want to *do* this?' Ron—." I looked away at nothing in particular, stalling— as if another minute would make the difference between grief and acceptance. "I *have* to do this." I turned back to face him, my head cocked a little sideways, the way I always did when I meant business. "I need for you to—I want you to know what it was like. That I wasn't making any of it up."

I heard myself *saying* the words, but it really sounded as if they came from someone else, they were so small and quiet. They trailed off— as if they lost the energy to make a sound.

"Anyway, thank you for coming, Ron. Not everyone— this is the sort of thing, well—I couldn't ask just *anyone* to do this."

"It's really dark..." he turned his head slightly and squinted, peering into my eyes. He looked precisely like Gregory Peck — Atticus Finch—so much so that it almost made you laugh because it was so uncanny. He had that way of peering into your soul, and his arched dark eyebrows gave him the visage of a wise man. It was a question he was asking rather than a statement of fact, still searching my resolve.

Right. Like I would be scared to go in because it was dark. What did he think I was, anyway—ordinary?

"I know the way—and I'm not scared either." I looked at him squarely, unflinchingly.

He nodded once in affirmation, respectfully, and we turned toward the house.

The driveway was on the left side of the house and it was only twelve steps or so- for a short person- to cross the flagstone path from the driveway to the front walkway that led up to the front porch. I glanced behind me to see if he was coming (and he was), and then rounding the right corner of the porch, headed toward the rear or the house. I knew the front door was locked.

I could hear his footsteps rustle in the deep and frozen leaves and snow behind me, his footsteps half as many as mine, for his stride made two of my own. We had worked together for months and gradually came to know that a friendship such as ours was a rare thing indeed. He was my supervisor, and through my conversations with both Ron and Toni, the other staff member in our small department, had told him a tale of something wonderful that took place behind the dark and somber façade of that broken house. Toni needed a miracle, and so did I. Maybe we all did. But in our efforts to really know each other and how we ought to pray through for the needs we had, I needed someone to know what I had lost.

I wondered what he thought. Was he sorry I'd talked him into coming here? Did he think I was crazy or was I actually remarkable? Was I just an eccentric flake, or was I a visionary? I felt that unless I was able to fully describe how it was and what had happened there that the whole experience would be lost forever. I needed an *objective* eye to observe what once was, so I would know I was not crazy. Finally I decided that he would have to make up his own mind on it, but the truth would speak for itself. What are friends for, anyway?

In the dim light from a streetlight I could see the peeling paint I'd started to scrape so long ago. Around the corner of the house we came. I had walked around that house a hundred times trimming and raking, planting and dreaming of future days.

"There's a cellar door here." I glanced back at him. "Oh, look, Ron! It's still unlocked."

I plucked away weeds and a tangle of grasses and pulled up on the wrought iron latch. The heavy cellar door creaked open. One of the tongue and groove boards fell right off as I raised the door to the vertical. Ron, with the gracefulness of a Zen master, caught it before it hit the ground. His reflexes were always agile and precise but strangely seemed in slow motion— it was always like watching a martial arts movie.

"Oh, don't worry," I apologized. "It always did that." I made a clumsy attempt to wedge it back into the space where the grooves were, but my fingers were so numb from the frigid winter night that I couldn't manage it. I gave up and laid the board on the sidewalk.

I looked up at him and asked if he was ready, but I was really only stalling until I gathered my nerve to descend into that dark cellar where anything from raccoons to feral cats could be waiting. So down into the darkness on narrow steps I trod, and he was right behind me.

Reaching the bottom of the stairs, I pushed the basement door open, disturbing long-abandoned spider's webs. The door scraped hard upon the concrete step. I stepped down one last step and into the darkness, across the damp floor where water had frozen in shining little rivulets on the cement, past the chairs in the corner, past the old suitcase with the hats in it, past the restaurant-grade Belgian waffle maker, and over to the stairs that led to the first floor and all the wonder of that old house.

"I'm surprised you can see," he said, from the darkness somewhere behind me.

"I can't, really. But I know this house like my own two hands. Oh, you should watch your head. The fellow who lived here before we did was tall also— he made these thingamajigs —look, he attached Styrofoam packing strips where every floor joist is."

Ron ducked under a joist and then a heating duct.

"Even if the door at the top of the stairs is locked, I have a skeleton key for it. See? It's still on my key chain." I held it up briefly and it dangled back and forth. "It was the only key that ever worked." I shoved it back into my coat pocket. In a way, the key to my house reminded me of a wedding ring, still worn by a grieving spouse, who was not yet ready to take it off.

We started up the basement stairs and I could see in the dim light that the door leading to the front hallway was open, just as I had left it!

We paused in the doorway from the basement to the foyer. Our breath hung in the air by the light of the streetlamp. It was certainly light enough to see since all of the trees that had once shaded the windows from the intrusive glare of the street lamps had been cut down when the Main Street (detonation) project began. There, in the blue-white light, everything was cold and damp and tomblike. And ju-u-st a little creepy.

I crossed the hallway and swung wide open the tall French doors of the living room. The release chain hung down and clapped rhythmically against the painted white woodwork of the door. Our footsteps echoed through the house and up the stairs as we walked across the rough dark wooden floors that had once welcomed so many. The boards creaked with our weight from the cold.

I could almost hear the walls, the floors, and the doors whispering to one another. "Look— she came back! She's *here!* The mistress of the house is— *home.*"

To Ron, I was certain the silent house seemed suspended in anticipation, waiting for a nameless destiny. It was only a house to him, I was sure. To me, it was where my heart and my years were spent. And everything in me was silently crying out that I would *never* have forgotten this dear house.

There was a bay window at the front of the house to the left as we walked into the living room, and to the right, were huge pocket doors. Through the window on the opposite wall from the French doors I could see our cars in the driveway.

"Red?"

"Hum? Oh—yes. This living room had been the color of coffee ice cream for much of the time we lived here— I painted it when we moved in. Emmy was only eight. But I painted it red about six months before we moved—it was November of last year. Except a little place above the French doors. I couldn't reach it because the computer was there, but then I had the accident before I could finish it. It was just beautiful though, Ron. You should have seen it at Christmas. The Christmas tree was here, in the bay as it always was. There was a cherry Queen Anne sideboard on that wall there— with a huge gold mirror above it. I had candles on it and greenery— and a huge bow on the mirror. It was grand. Dickens himself would have been proud. There was pine roping and burgundy velvet bows and white lights around the doors of the foyer and on the banister all the way up."

I walked through a narrow opening between the pocket doors. Closing my eyes, I could still hear them roll like thunder on the track above. Daughters would always part them like curtains when they wanted some "time with mom". I would be reading, or just sitting with a cup of coffee, and then I would hear the doors rumble and glance over to see Abbie or Emmy slip in between them.

"Do they work?"

"Sure they do. See?" I pushed the heavy doors, rumbling and complaining on their track, back into the wall and the living room and study became one huge room.

"Fireplace?"

"Mm hum. Actually, this was my room when we first moved in here. I put candles in the fireplace to make believe it really worked. When I decided to make the house into the café, I took my bed down and put it out in the garage and then I just slept on my loveseat. I decided I would need the whole downstairs to do the coffeehouse right."

"I see. For three *years*?"

"Well, my thinking was that lots of missionaries spend time in prison and sleep on the floor of a jail cell for *their* ministry. It seemed like a small price to pay.

"I had looked at so many houses before I found this one. I knew I would know the right house when I saw it." I fingered the latch of the pocket door.

"The night we moved in, I remember I sat on the living room floor, leaning against the wall with boxes all around, and cried. There had been times that I thought we — my children and I—would end up homeless.

"It had been such a long journey — searching for just the right house, though I guess at the time I didn't know that I was looking for a house that would be a part of my destiny. I was so very grateful for this house and for all the things I had been given I couldn't keep it all to myself. I mean, I had to find a way to share with other people what I could never have gotten all on my own. I'm not the type of person who works their whole life to build a little empire that I can keep all to myself. I was never about buying expensive vehicles and status trappings. It's okay to have nice things, but I wanted to somehow share what I had with other people. Upholstery will wear out and dishes will break, but it is the times of friendship and camaraderie and the sharing of our lives over those cups and saucers that lasts a lifetime. Anyway, sometimes it seems as if the only way to express your thanks to God is to offer back the gifts you've been given and to share them. A great movie is always more fun if someone you know shares it with you."

He was nodding in agreement, his hand resting on the bookshelf.

"Come on. I'll show you the kitchen— you'll love it".

We crossed the room and went through another door to the left of the fireplace.

"This was the dining room. I had the most wonderful chandelier— when I turned it down low, the frosted globes glowed a warm gold in the center of the room just above the table— the table was a lovely sugar maple, and it glowed just like sunlight through honey— it was just lit up with the lamplight. It was the most unusual light, and all the corners of the room melted into darkness. It was so merry at the table with all of us sitting around it at dinner—and on Saturday nights this room seemed to be the gathering point, and folks would carry in chairs from other rooms. Late into the night we talked, sometimes only a few people were here— three or four, especially when it was really snowy outside. It was a time for confidences— and telling of our life's dreams and secrets."

We stood again in silence.

To the left again we turned and we were in the small kitchen. The winter moon, so bright and full, was rising above the bare black limbs and branches and shone through the large window to our right—the rear of the house. She cast her moonlight, bright and luminescent, across the white floor. The whole room glowed as if it emanated it's *own* light. I remembered watching the moon rise on a winter evening just like this, coming up over the top of the carriage house and through the frozen branches, watching the stars join her before I turned on the lamp that was always on the kitchen table. She was *my* moon, my nighttime friend; a gift from God, to light up the edges of the night clouds.

I crossed from the doorway to the counter on the opposite wall. "I *loved* these white cabinets with all their little glass panes— and e*spec*ially this little window here above the sink."

I reached up and touched the panes of the cabinets, as I had so many times done, and my fingertips lingered there, afraid the little panes would vanish into thin air if I took them away. *"Am I really here in this house again— touching these cabinet doors I loved so well?"* I thought. *"Or am I only dreaming I'm here?"*

I had been so homesick, and now I was home. Only it was not *my* home anymore, but belonged to someone who was yet to buy it. A nameless person with an obscure face, whose identity was a mystery yet to me would have what I had loved and lost. Would the new owner be a mercenary scoundrel, fixing it up just enough to sell it and make a killing—or would they love her as I had? This dear house, the scene of so many celebrations and tragedies, was in a purgatory all its own called Foreclosure.

"See how the little window here in the middle matches the cabinets? I would unfasten this little latch and open it when I did dishes. In summer I could watch the birds and hear children playing make-believe next door. In winter the morning sun would shine through this frosted window when it first came up, all pink and golden. It made the *whole kitchen* brilliant rose colored! I would wait for the coffee to brew and stand here in the glory of it. I loved the wallpaper— all the tiny leaves. All the wallpaper here is exactly what I would have picked— it was as if the house was waiting for me. It was as if the house loved me before ever I loved it

"We watched the season's come and go, and watched the kittens grow up. I sat in here in the dark with my coffee on winter mornings, keeping perfect company with the last of the moonlight and with a fuzzy blanket around my shoulders, my coffee cup warming my hands. I would watch the snow falling like feathers from grandma's best bed pillows. Down through all the trees, lining them the way no artist could—"

I paused, and then turned to Ron.

It was so hard — being there, and yet not *living* there, though, truth be known, I never thought I'd set foot in it again. I had planned on living there until the girls were grown, until I was an old woman whose house would be a wonderland for grandchildren to visit. I would be an old woman, with roses by the door and lemonade on the front porch. I would be an old woman with a lifetime of wonder in that house.

I would have been an old woman there but for all that happened that I was powerless to stop. One obstacle I could have overcome, but not an endless bombardment of downsizings (three in four years), repairs and misfortune. The only choice I really had in the face of all of it was to fight back by doing something dazzlingly heroic.

Kinda like artfully arranging the china settings on the tables of the *Titanic*.

"I used to think, sitting here at the table on Christmas Day 'There have been a hundred and ten years that this old house saw. One hundred and ten Octobers where the sun fell upon the floor there and against the wall, when the smell of fallen leaves in the rain came through that window —one hundred ten Junes, where the sunlight swept across the walls of the dining room. One hundred ten Christmas Eves, when wrapping paper, crisp and crinkling, was concealing many a secret kept well—and one hundred ten Christmas mornings.' I bet this old house waited for *each one* of those days, lovingly, just as I did."

I could always talk that way to Ron. I never had to hide what I was thinking. Ron was the sort that could handle the truth of how folk felt, no matter *how* they felt. Many were the people in the large international ministry where I worked who had come to confide their fears and hopes in Ron. He was like an early church saint, wise and gentle. Few people are that big inside.

I wanted to change the subject.

"Don't you love old hardware? The little *clicking* sounds it makes when you turn a knob— or fasten a latch." I pretended I was good at the duck and dodge, changing the subject. I paused and my voice trailed off. I opened the cabinet door and then pushed it slowly shut, awaiting the efficient, cheerful 'click'.

"Have you ever noticed that they will tear down a lovely old farmhouse—or cannibalize it to a salvage shop—and throw a hundred subdivision houses into the field where the old farmhouse once stood—and then put brass "vintage" drawer pulls on the drawers in the subdivision house that they bought brand new at the local home improvement store? It's as if they don't value the *real* thing enough to preserve it, but tear it down and then scramble around trying to make the new look vintage, or 'classic'."

We stood there in the dark at that big window. I would never look out at the black branches lined with new-fallen snow, never see the moon shining through those same trees on a summer night when she called you out into her lovely blue-white light and you were coaxed there by her magic in nightgown like a gossamer moth, where you raise your hands in praise to God who made the moon just so.

I turned away.

"Let's go upstairs." I mumbled.

We made our way through the dining room and back into the front hallway— a complete circle— and started up the twisted stairway. Up two steps to the landing. To the right was a small square stained glass window that cast amber and rose-colored squares on the wall. It looked out upon the front porch and the small yard.

"Look at this. This is the house number in the middle: 417. It was painted by the man who built the house— he was a house and sign painter by trade, and his wife was a schoolteacher-Lucille Blackburn was her name. In all one hundred ten years, no one has disturbed this window. See the gold leaf paint that fell down between the panes? If anyone had tried to "fix" it, it would never be the same window again."

We continued up the stairs. At the top was another landing —a turn to the left and three more stairs to the small square hallway. There had been a leak in the roof where the gables met and the water and ice had dammed and came in. A large chunk of plaster had fallen and shattered on the hardwood floor.

"This was Maureen's and Emmy's room here at the front of the house. When Maureen went to Atlanta for a year in the ministry, Emmy had it all to herself. Sometimes she was afraid of the dark and would ask me to sleep in her bed. She was ten, and really quite brave most of the time. And this was Lisa and Abby's room. They started to take off the wallpaper because they said it reminded them of beef stroganoff—the color and the pattern. Who else but a kid will say something is the color of beef stroganoff? They never got a chance to finish it — I think it was more a case of biting off more than they could chew. Sometimes when we would leave to go to church or on a trip, Emmy would say, 'Goodbye, house!'. Sometimes I even said it myself. It was like the house was a person we loved and who loved us back."

It was supposed to be lighthearted, but it all had a hollow sound. My throat ached but that was nothing compared to my heart.

"This was the bathroom. It was originally a bedroom, but when they put the plumbing inside, they turned it into a bathroom."

"It's *huge*!" Ron remarked. "Even with the tub placed diagonally."

"I know! All *five* of us—six if my son Michael came up to visit— could be in here talking and getting ready to go somewhere—you now, just carrying on, and annoying one another, and there was still room. The only problem was that it was so big it never got warm from the steam, so in winter it was just awfully chilly. It really needed a fireplace"

He walked over to the shuttered window. He was so tall he could see above the shutters down into the yard next door.

"That's Miss Maisy's." I offered.

"It looks like a park! Wait! What in the world is *that*? It looks—"

"Like a windmill?"

"Yes!"

"The year before that she had a wishing-well built. It is already a gift to the whole neighborhood. It would always be Stillwell Place to other people, but *we'll* always call it Miss Maisy's. I would always see her tending her flowers. I want to have that much imagination when I get older. She is the perfect example of growing older gracefully."

We stood there in the dark. The silence crept in the bathroom door and crouched there in the corners of the room.

I turned and went out into the hall, past the chunk of plaster and started down the stairs, hearing each footfall on the wooden treads, knowing exactly which ones would creak, sliding my hand over the rail where greenery circled and burgundy bows punctuated every fourth step at Yuletide. I paused at the bottom landing, and looked through the clear segments of the stained glass window. So many times I stood there looking at the snow falling after saying final goodnights and prayers for the girls. I also kept a watchful eye on their beaus, as the porch swing was just below the window.

Ron followed down the stairs and stood behind me. I turned and placed my hand on the newel post.

"There's money in here." I said, making light of it. "Thirty-seven cents. We put it there when we first moved here, just so we could say there was money in it. Emmy was eight years old at the time."

I pulled the finial off the top and kissed it as George Bailey had done in *"It's a Wonderful Life"* quoting, "Hello, you wonderful drafty old house!"

I turned on the landing and went down the two final steps, standing before the front door. There was still a lace curtain at the window above the door's mail slot.

I wanted to show him that the doorbell was really a real live *bell*, attached by a rivet that allowed a visitor to ring it by hand. It always had such a cheerful sound. I halted, my hand on the door knob.

"I've been running, and I just can't run anymore." I thought.

Suddenly I felt that familiar sick dread that had been my constant companion for most of the four years we had lived there. I felt as if *I* was holding up the house, the fish-scale shingles painted purple, the window over the sink, the little cubby hole door under the eves, the fallen plaster, the leaking roof—as if the weight of the last century, and all that had happened there in that house was collapsing in on itself like a dying star.

I was running from the loss of a dream-come-true like some will run from death. For me, they were one and the same.

Most of the time I had lived there that dread had haunted me, had awakened me in the tiny hours before dawn, when only the ticking of the many little clocks and the light of the moon were my company. How could something that I—not to mention so many others—had loved so much have been the source of such heartache? It was silent again and I felt that we were in mortal danger of drowning in it.

Why had I brought him here, to this empty old derelict house anyway? I was angry with myself for being sentimental, and for making him feel as if he had to come along. But I had told him so much about what happened here and I needed an objective eye, someone who had not been a friend of The Open Door Cafe to see that something really special had happened in the house that stood silently in the cold of a December night.

I turned and looked through the hallway and beyond it into the dining room to the back door and the carriage house beyond the door. When we had lived there, there were candles and the glow of lamplight. There was always Irish music and the chatter of daughters, the teasing of a visiting son, and the scampering of our Westie. Everywhere I looked, I saw it as if there was a camera's flash, and in the flash was the instantaneous image of "How It Was" for a split second— and then all was dimmed into the cold and dark reality of what now was. *Flash!* My daughter standing at the foot of the stairs with her beautiful and mischievous grin. *Flash!* The Tiffany lamp and the Waterford bowl on the table with the cabriole legs. *Flash!*

Emmy at eight years old nestled in the corner of the sofa with her book of fairy tales.

And in between the flashes of memory, in the dark and cold, there were papers scattered on the floor and Popsicle sticks from neighbor children who had gotten in— and the painting of the red living room that was left unfinished because a car accident just three weeks before we moved rendered my arms almost useless for months. Standing there, I could see both the past and the present at once.

The sadness was suffocating.

"It wasn't really like this, you know" my voice sounded thin and distant, like it was coming to my own ears from far away.

"Ron?" I looked up at his face, bent down towards mine. "This— all of this is only darkness and shadows— and the blasted cold! But there was a beautiful secretary there with Beleek china and my hammered dulcimer was here and the music filled this place! People loved for me to play it on Saturday nights and I played them Irish tunes. Some of them danced and everyone clapped in time to the music. There were candles and the whole *house* glowed. There were so many times we laughed until we cried, and made cookies at Christmas and presents too. Maureen met her husband while we lived here. The girls always could tell when I came home and they would come running down these stairs to ask about supper and to tell me about school. Their friends called me Marmie after the mother in *Little Women*. We were just like that. And *hundreds* of total strangers came through this very door, Ron— and found a home here. I knew them all by name. I know it doesn't look it, but it really was magic. Can't you *see* it?" I urged helplessly, wanting desperately for him to see that the house, this house—was not the desolate cave it seemed, but that there was once a light that filled the whole of it.

I looked up at him, my dear and faithful friend, maybe one of the few people in my life that *really* knew me. I knew it was okay to feel everything I was feeling and couldn't even name. All the years of hardship and uncertainty raising my children by myself, trying to give them gifts no one could ever see wrapped in ribbons, but gifts that only the most discerning people would perceive; all the nights of wondering what would become of us; all the times I realized how blessed I was just to have my family safe, looking at their faces across from me at the dinner table. It all rushed in like a terrible storm crashing down.

"God, I know why a ghost will haunt a place!" I sobbed into my hands

The grief of leaving it forever in the darkness of the winter night, all alone— when it had been so well loved by so very many — not the least of all myself— left me powerless, and my arms just dropped to my sides. If you don't have heart, you just can't fight anymore.

I leaned forward against Ron's fuzzy sweatshirt, the zipper scratching my face, and he hugged me there in the stillness of the old house—*our* old house, my children's and mine—the twenty-ninth house I'd looked at, the one that stole my heart, the one that spoke volumes to me the moment I crossed the threshold.

"Let it go." he encouraged. "Just let it go."

At that moment I realized that I was crying not for the loss of the house. The house was only the most *recent* of enormous losses and terrors. I wept for all the times I hadn't the luxury of tears, when being strong for the sake of my children meant that I didn't have time to feel sad for all that had happened. I wept for the baby that died that I was not permitted to grieve and would never know as a young woman, for the life I *could* have led if only I had just a *little* help. I didn't need a lot of help— just a little. I wept for the absence of just a *little* help when I needed it most.

But mostly I wept for the terrible *beauty* that encompassed all of it, the sadness and the joy, the terror and the triumph. I wept at the knowledge of the vast story this house and all who came here told through my life, and for how what happened to me could mean hope for someone else who likewise struggled. I wept for everyone who had a story just like mine— and who would never have a chance to tell it—for everyone who had overcome dark and terrifying things against all the odds. I wept at leaving part of myself behind—there in the silent darkness on that December night, there in that charming Victorian with its peeling raspberry sherbet pink paint and the little white six-paned window above the sink, the little window where I watched October glow crimson and gold. I had decorated it like an artist paints a canvas, placing everything just so, and now the canvas was in shreds.

What had happened there was unique and unparalleled, the stuff great stories are made of and God was telling it through someone small and yet courageous, who kept hoping for a miracle.

But most of all, I knew that the light that had filled that old house was not the *house's* light at all. It was *our* light— the light that was my family, the courage we had, the love we had shared, and the memories we made; a light that came from terrible hardship and was forged into an eternal light by the fires we had walked through. The light that drew people there was that spirit of courage and gallows humor, of determination to make the best of times in the worst of times.

We were the light— *I* was the light.

That may have been the hardest thing to face, that I had been running from the goodness in my own self that inspired me to make a sacred place for all the people who didn't *have* a sacred place. I realized in an instant that there really was something wonderful in me, forged in brokenness and that wonderful, heavenly light, the light that illuminated the house, was found in the ashes of who I *had been*, and who I had *become*.

After a while, I felt so tired and strangely at peace. Like an abandoned child who had come to grips with the way things were and stopped pretending things could ever change, but gathered up their spirit to take on the world as a big adventure— I came to a point of acceptance. I felt that I had wrestled the dark thing to the ground. I had lost it all in the process, but had gained something else there in that hallway. I had learned a great lesson.

Ron stepped back, and bending to the side looked at my face. A royal mess, I was.

"I'm ruint." I said, trying to wipe my eyes.

"What?" he leaned down closer to hear.

"Ruint-it's West Virginian for 'ruined'."

He chuckled and hugged me. And then leaning down, his hand on the doorknob, looked again at me. The familiar click of the latch and the reflection of the wavy glass as it swept across the walls of the hallway and the French doors as the front door swung open. I remembered standing in the dark hallway when the last guest left on a Saturday night, closing the front door and turning off the porch light after watching the last of them get into their cars and drive away.

"It really was grand." I said. "I wish you could have been here."

"I know it was," he answered, smiling kindly. "I can almost see it."

"*Really?*"

"Oh, most *assuredly.*" He was famous for that phrase.

I nodded, looking down.

He paused respectfully. "Ready?" I nodded.

We walked out onto the front porch and down the two steps to the front walkway, where the white arbor, embellished with hundreds of white lights at Christmas, had once been. I smiled thinking that I wished for my daughters' first kisses to take place under that brilliant arbor. I turned to face the porch, with the turquoise and purple door dimly visible by streetlamp. I remembered when lights glowed in every window, and how I had saved the first leaves I had raked there.

"Goodbye, house." I whispered.

Chapter 2

I am often asked what on earth gave me the notion to start a coffee house in my home. The only thing I can think of to tell them was that the notion wasn't actually *of* this Earth.

It was in October, the *best* of months, when first I opened my door to total strangers. With the aching of autumn fever enveloping the trees and the dampness of the old house, the very air was full of the stillness of the season on the verge of sleeping. The crickets were few and solitary, and the seasonal cicadas had ceased their rhythmic singing. The air, warm and balmy during the day, sighed with the coming of twilight and the cool damp evening clung to the anticipation of frost in the days to come, clung to the last breaths of summer. The onset of early autumn is a bittersweet comfort.

How shall I describe how it was, there in that house, that raspberry pink Victorian on Main Street — the magic of a Saturday night at The Open Door Café with the voices, the tinkling of glasses and the aroma of spicy incense and the nutty full aroma of coffee in the air? And that *hundreds* of people, complete strangers each with their *own* story to tell, walked across my threshold and stepped into a lifelong dream.

Do not think that it was so odd a thing to do, for it all followed on the heels of a journey through such trials of faith and triumph that even *I* find it hard to believe that it all really did happen once upon a time.

It all began in a little town in the heart of the heartland. It used to be the kind of town one passed through on their way to Somewhere

Else. *Any*-where Else. Time forgot it— along with a lot of other people— until a hundred men with vision (they called themselves The Hundred Thousand-Dollar Club) chipped in a thousand dollars each, and one-by-one bought up the dilapidated, tired old buildings. They refurbished them, preserving their bygone charm to remind us of what we came from— that Pioneer Stock we've always been told was our heritage.

It is now the kind of town everybody *wishes* they came from. Where downtown is about eight blocks from most anywhere.

There's a bell tower atop the Town Hall and a bandstand on the Town Square. Tourists come to try to forget that they live in the big city, and that their lives have become chained to a day-planner and a cell phone.

If you were to walk down Broadway, through "the central business district" (of only three and a half blocks), and where any one of the shop owners you meet would know you by name, you would almost feel that time forgot the place. The heart just beats a little slower here. There is the Dickens' Bookstore here and the drug store over there, across the street. In summer, even on a day with low humidity, inside most of the buildings there is the unmistakable smell of *Old*.

On the corner stands the stately— and, might I add— tastefully shabby Golden Lamb Inn, where it is boasted that Charles Dickens slept on more than one occasion, as well as Samuel Langhorne Clemens, Harriet Beecher Stowe, and *even* six Presidents. At two hundred years old, it is one of the few businesses that a ninety-six year old can remember visiting as a youngster—and even *then* it was just plain old. Next to the inn there is a small and pristine park with brick walkways, petunias and geraniums galore, and a bandstand, too, surrounded by flowers. Weddings are held there. And every Thursday evening in summertime there are free concerts sponsored by the Rotarians.

Three doors down there is a shop with a red and white awning. The huge window with divided panes brightens even the dreariest winter day. "Village Ice Cream Shop"says the sign in ornate white letters against a deep blue background above the red and white striped awning. Sitting inside at a table by that bright window, you will see above the pristine white crocheted café curtains the first snow flurries of winter and in summer the ominous dark purple clouds of a thunderstorm. The flooring is the same type of small octagon-shaped ceramic tiles that were on great grandma's bathroom floor. The menu rarely changes, but then, no one seems to tire of it. After all, it has become The Place You Go. You go there to share an afternoon with your daughter struggling through the growing pains of being fifteen; you go there with company; you go there with a date, and to console a broken heart. You conduct the business of life there over a lemon soda, and celebrate the little victories of living day by day.

Street after street is lined with old homes; massive, multi-colored Victorians (you have to have at *least* three colors on a Victorian) and Gothic cottages decorated with wicker and hanging baskets, where croquet was once played on the expansive lawns, and lemonade served on the porch. Great oaks, maples and the gracious sycamore trees, nicknamed *the ghosts of the forest* with their dappled gray and white bark, are like cavernous cathedrals.

Every street is shaded by old trees that have outgrown the sidewalks, bulging over the warped concrete as if they melted there. There is something comforting in the determination of Nature to prevail, in the seedling that sprouts between the cracks in the sidewalk of the inner city or in the ability of a wren to find a nesting place to shelter in the eaves of the starkest building. And so it is that the buckling of a sidewalk by a great crimson maple seems to me the kindest intrusion of Nature.

In September, just after the first chilly mornings of autumn, the town hosts the Apple Festival. All the shopkeepers move out of doors with their wares and the air is filled with the aroma of barbecue, funnel cakes, and roasted nuts. Beekeepers display jar after jar of honey, apple butter and homemade jelly and preserves. There are wagon rides and pony rides. Police officers on bicycles laugh and gesture with the old men. The ladies from the church near the high school have made *huge* apple dumplings—"a meal in themselves!" they will tell you—and you can resign yourself to gladly spoiling your dinner. There are strains of Irish melodies from a hammered dulcimer on one corner, and a barbershop quartet — or a brass band —on another.

In December, this whole scene is revisited, only the air is full of snowflakes dancing wildly on the crisp and fragrant winter wind and your breath is in the air. There is a merry anticipation in the air and it is swirling with the snow. The aroma of doughnuts fried in a huge kettle and roasting nuts coaxes a smile from even the grumpiest Scrooge. And the tourists, captivated by the whole unbridled merriment of the scene, imagine themselves to be Back Then, in those very days, when here in this little town Dickens himself once walked.

When evening falls, and the sun, all golden, rose and crimson, begins to slip down behind the far away ridge lined with frozen black branches, people begin to gather at the curb. At one end of Broadway there can be seen the beginning of what looks like fireflies. Little by little they spread southward; both sides of the street sparkle with the flames of thousands of candles, each wick kindled by the dancing flame of another's candle and held in mittened and red-fingered hands.

Thousands of people line the streets, tall folk behind and we smaller folk in front— to await the largest parade of horse-drawn antique carriages and sleds in the country. It's *all* here in this parade, ladies and gents. We have Arabians and *the* Clydesdales, elegant and mysterious French Percherons of black, miniature ponies and mules, not to mention horse-drawn fire trucks, child-sized wagons, and vintage sleds, driven merrily and with great flourishing gestures by men and women in top hats and bustles.

It is on Main Street, just four blocks away from the bustle of this business district, that there stands a quaint small Victorian, or more accurately, a Queen Anne. As someone said of it once, "Her makeup is a little smeared, but she's a beauty". She's deep raspberry-sherbet pink with purple fish-scale shingles on the upper portion, and bright turquoise shutters. Hardly any other combination would accentuate the many angles to her, and the fact that she is looking just a tiny bit shabby, with the paint peeling a little on the east and south sides, only accentuates her charm.

She's quirky, but she's a looker.

It is the kind of house that people would *name*— out of sheer affection— just as they did in bygone days with the stately residences of New England and Britain.

All had loved her well, and some folks called her "Annie".

There are little windows in odd places; more windows show on the outside than you can count on the inside. They were in the strangest of places— in closets, in attics, over stairways. Whimsy took precedence over practicality in those days. They made no cookie-cutter houses then. Oh, *no*...

They made *gingerbread* houses.

The house is surrounded by huge trees, as most of the gracious old homes on the street are, and the magenta redbud trees that in spring seemed to be intentionally painted on this postcard picture house to coordinate perfectly in hue, in autumn form a deep claret drapery of heart-shaped leaves against her vivid raspberry pink. The front yard is nothing more than a small flowerbed and is planted in ivy, perennials and vivid mums in deep russet, magenta, gold and orange. People will pause when taking their walk and look at the lavish profusion of blossoms and herbs there. A flagstone path curves in a half circle from the narrow driveway on one side, edged in beacon silver. At evening time, the landscape lights shown through the foliage and glowed in variegated green in a semi-circle from the driveway to the corner of the porch.

Over the short front walkway which leads from the sidewalk up to the front porch, there is a white arbor, complete with a little rounded-top gate, the latch of which is always temperamental, as if it wants to stay open but people keep on insisting it be closed. In summer, clematis on one side tries to compete with ivy from the other to climb the arbor (I think the ivy is winning).

The tradition is, the first time someone visits, they have to go through the arbor and gate. After that, they can just use the stone path around it. Those who come calling always fiddle with the latch then start to walk around. If I were watching, I would come to the front door, tongue in cheek, and tell them of the tradition and without fail, laughing, they would always go back around and come through the gate.

They were family then.

Through the white arbor you go and just five strides up the front walkway, spring up two steps, and you're on the front porch. To the right of the front door, there is a small bench from the original carriage house covered in three layers of old peeling paint. In autumn, pumpkins and mums will take a seat there and corn stalks will stand guard in the left corner by the front door. In winter a child's pair of old white ice skates and a sled will rest there between sprigs of Emmy and pine. To the right of the turquoise and purple door, there is a small square stained glass window— and in the center is ornately painted the number

417

—it was painted, in fact, by the original owner who was a house and sign painter by trade. He and his wife, a schoolteacher, built the house in 1890. Some of the gold leaf paint has flaked over time and has accumulated in a little pile beneath the numbers— and because it is sandwiched between two panes, it has been undisturbed it in all 112 years that the house has stood.

Two small white cottage chairs with the white paint likewise worn and peeling stand beside the bench for the occasional visitors who "just stopped by for a moment"—and end up leaving an hour and a half-glass of lemonade later. There is a wooden screen door held loosely shut by an old spring closure and the sound of it stretching wide and the resulting CLAP! CLAP CLAP... is the sound of company coming, and the girls coming home from school.

It is altogether charming and full of comfort. And most of all, it is not some scene wishfully invented for the sake of a good story. It is real and only four and a half blocks from where I presently live.

Our tale begins here, then, in this oasis from the march of time. It begins in this beloved old house—*my* house. Here, behind this turquoise and purple door with its lace curtain—the door that I opened to so many *hundreds of total strangers*— began a dream, as all good tales do. It was the dream of doing something remarkable, uncommon, and maybe even a little heroic. Of risking the security of the habitual because I dared wonder what it would feel like to accomplish the unthinkable.

So begins this journey of healing, of wonder, of trials and faith, with the regulars, the *Friends,* of The Open Door Café.

Chapter 3

They call it downsizing; right sizing, or "restructuring" and it has many causes. But it always means pretty much the same thing.
Laid off.
It was a very gradual thing, but I found that my position was slowly being phased out. Following a labor strike by the parts division of one of the major auto manufacturers, the car dealership where I had worked for almost five years was cutting back (most folks don't know that a car dealership really makes money in what is called Fixed Operations, that is, Parts, Body Shops and Service — selling cars only insures that there is a steady stream of cars to fix). Many dealerships nationwide had gone out of business— after all, if you don't have the parts to fix the cars with, you can't stay in business very long.
The dealership where I worked had simply cut back. Which *sounds* benign enough until the cutback has, among its casualties, a single mother with a name and an address. Where I had once organized public relations events and coordinated community service initiatives, and acted as a mediator and negotiator for customers with issues, I found myself driving the Courtesy Shuttle for the Service Department. Though an ancient Chinese proverb says, "*All* work is honorable", I felt that there was so much more I *could* be doing, but wasn't doing. Would my skills and talents gradually atrophy until I forgot that I had them at all? Was I *settling for* coasting along, my life on cruise control, adrift in circumstances?

I knew for certain that I did not want to live my life merely reacting to life, but to have charted my course and lived with intent. There is a *very* big difference, my friend. The trouble is, I couldn't seem to define what my course should be. Was *I* to determine my course, or did something with a different name beckon from just beyond my view?

I felt increasingly as if I had to do, well—*something*. The problem was, I didn't have any idea what the something was.

There is a quote by Frederick Bruechner in his work, *Wishful Thinking, A Theological ABC:* "The place God calls you to is the place where *your deep gladness* and the *world's deep hunger meet.*"

That's it!

Our *raison d'être* is to find the thing we most desire to do and brings us the most profound joy— *and* which also meets a great need in others.

I was haunted by an incident that had happened once. It was one of those life-changing mental pictures you carry around in your head like it was a picture in your wallet.

Years before, a co-worker and I were shredding old files to make room for new ones. Drawer after drawer of files— representing year after year in the lives of the people who had worked there and had done business there— went through the shredder. I looked at some of the names. Some of them I didn't know— hadn't known in the five years I'd worked there. One salesman had been killed in a car accident. The files represented years in these peoples' lives—years that had known marriages, divorces, the birth of a first child, and the death of a parent.

All this effort, all this—this *life*— represented in these stacks of files, was eventually shredded by a paper shredder and amounted to nothing more than seven large clear plastic bags of confetti. My co-worker had stepped away for a few minutes. I stared at the plastic bags slumped on their sides and The Bigger, Deeper Meaning remained long after they landed in the Dumpster. And as I drove the Courtesy Shuttle mile after mile, I wondered if this was the fruit of my life, the motorized version of confetti. Was this all that my life amounted to?

After weeks (which then turned into *months*) of praying for direction, knowing that the shuttle-driver position would end when the regular driver came back, I realized that God wasn't giving me any direction, even though I had a feeling of being on The Edge of Something Big. There was no overtime to be had at work, and I realized that I was at a point of diminishing returns. I would be getting farther behind in my mortgage. Projecting ahead four months, I knew it would all be over. I came to the conclusion that I would actually make more if I cared for children in my home. At least that way I would be there with my own children instead of being separated by a freeway-turned-obstacle-course with a construction project on I-71 and a constant traffic jam.

But it was more than a financial bogeyman I was wrestling. It involved something I was unable to describe, and it was bigger than I was. It was something like… Destiny.

"There just has to be more to a lifetime than this." I thought. I needed to feel as if what I was spending my time doing was having meaning beyond the moment— some eternal value. Months before, I would *never* have had the longing of doing anything more than what I was already doing. I was happy with my job. I was in the groove. When I wasn't resolving customer concerns I was helping organize the next big event which usually meant hosting open houses and preparing food and serving large numbers of people in no time flat. And, to be really honest, I was really pretty self-absorbed. I wasn't obnoxious about it, but like a lot of you reading this, *I* was at the helm of my life, and I knew it just wasn't enough. I wanted something that would stretch me in areas of my life that I needed to grow in.

Driving the courtesy shuttle for months, I had had plenty of time to think, mostly in silence. And the nagging thought kept coming, "Is this all there is?" It became so strong that I thought even if I was doing my *former* job, my eyes had been opened to yet another possibility— a larger, deeper, broader possibility. The calling, the wooing of the Lover of my very soul, seemed so much stronger than the empty lure of a career.

Wasn't there *some* way I could use what I knew best to serve the One I loved most?

Sometimes my passenger in the courtesy shuttle was a fellow-Christian and we would talk about the call of God. Was it always to be a missionary in a far away land, or on the streets of the inner city? Or was it broader than that? Maybe the call of God is living in such a way that He is the one people see when they look at our eyes, or hear kind words from our heart—it is not *working* at ministry, but rather *living* it. It is easy to see this in the life of Mother Theresa— though I could never compare myself to her.

When my oldest daughter, Maureen (sometimes we called her Peggy), was three, she would sit on my lap and look up at my face with such delight—she would lean forward and peer into my eyes so intently, and say, "I see *Peggy* in your eyes!" For the longest time, I thought she meant that she could see how much I loved her. But then I realized that she really was seeing her own reflection in my eyes. But it was because she was so focused on the face of her mother, and I was so caught up in the moment with my child it was really possible to look that closely, that intently, and see herself reflected in the tiny pupils there. "Seeing Peggy" meant *both* things.

Was the call of God to be such a person that others would see Him reflected from our eyes and know how much He loves them? Does He see *Himself* reflected there?

The picture of the plastic bags of confetti came to my mind many times, and eventually it became clear that I was going to have to bid farewell to what I affectionately called The Confetti-Mobile. The relentless beckoning of a greater destiny collided head on with the return of the regular driver and I knew I needed to find something else. My former job had been eliminated. I penned my resignation letter and when my final day came there was a grand party (interpretation: *wake*) — something that they reserved for people who retired. The company president, the one *I* had always admired, and who had taught me so many principles that later guided me in my endeavors— read letters from people who had written to the dealership about the effect I had had on their lives. One woman had written to tell of a time when I stopped to pick her up after her car, a newer model sport utility, had broken down on the expressway. I had passed the car and saw her in the distance walking. Of course I pulled over and offered her a ride— wouldn't *anyone*? Granted, she probably got in because "Courtesy Shuttle" was emblazoned on the side, which eliminated the likelihood that I was an axe murderer. I gave her a ride to the dealership since her car was one of the models we serviced. She was able to call a tow truck and afterwards I took her over to a nearby hotel —within walking distance of the dealership. She told him in the letter that if ever there was an angel of the dealership it was me. Now, I felt that I was only doing the right thing, but with tears in his eyes he proclaimed me to be "the Dealership Angel".

WHAT? Who were they talking about anyway? I had *no idea* that people thought of me that way. But it was Robert Burns who wrote, "Oh, what a gift as God would gie us, to see oursel's as others see us". I was only doing what seemed the natural thing to do, what was my reasonable service, what *any* caring person would do, without regard to whether I appeared old fashioned, corny or, as my children refer to it, a Dork. After all, we aren't supposed to act like barbarians, are we? I wasn't one to care if it seemed odd that I would do a good deed for a stranger on the street, or even pay for the person's groceries in line in front of me at the grocery store. I loved the reckless abandonment of doing a good deed completely out of the blue. After all, isn't that what *He* would do if He were down here? I needed the approval of no one but God, and if He was pleased with me, well, I was okay with that.

For some indefinable reason, I was compelled to take a lesser role, *to become smaller to myself.* Somehow, I knew that in the economy of God, *less is actually more.* Being smaller in my own eyes meant I could be bigger for other people. The odd thing is, qualities were emerging in me that were different than what is valued in the business world; a sense of compassion, the willingness to help and serve others, and the way I tried to encourage the people who were struggling.

Funny, not one person mentioned I was good at adding numbers together or making a high volume of phone calls, that I had sold them a car or resolved their consumer concern. When it came down to it, the job performance that mattered most was the quality of being a fellow human being with compassion, and someone who could meet the needs of someone else.

So... here I am writing this, and I'm wondering if you, dear reader, know how people see *you?* Are you aware of how you influence the lives of others —even without your knowledge? Are you aware the people really are watching you? Like myself, are you unaware that your seemingly small good deed may actually be a Big Deal to someone else who *needs* the good deed?

I was a little nervous about leaving my "secure" job, but also excited about the possibilities that lay ahead. I was reasonably prepared to hold out a few months until something materialized. I had some savings in the form of two 401K plans—not a whole lot, but enough to sustain my family still at home and myself for about five months.

So I loaded the remainder of the cake and the bouquets of flowers into my Subaru and headed home... to "pursue some entrepreneurial endeavors" —which *sounded* great in my resignation letter. How could I tell them I felt God was calling me to do Something Else, and I didn't really know what the "something else" was? Instead of pursuing entrepreneurial endeavors, it felt suspiciously like jumping off of a cliff into a fog-shrouded abyss.

So this is what living by faith is? It always sounds very brave and heroic, and *oh,* so noble and spiritual. *"You can't fool me, Lord"*, I thought. *"They call this walking by faith, but it's really The Fog-Shrouded Abyss Thing, isn't it?"*

Like many of you, I went to church and sang all the great praise and worship songs. It was all very comfortable. I was in the groove. Then one Sunday morning, though I always had meant the words I was singing, because of my growing restlessness and the certain conviction that I was about to embark on a real life adventure, and for a reason I didn't even know, I was drawn forward into a place in worship I'd never been. Tears ran down my cheeks, against my will. This really wasn't my usual mode of worship. Something was up– and it had His fingerprints all over it.

I knew something was happening that God was orchestrating. I knew full well at that moment that there would be a price to pay to get to where I knew He was calling me to go. But at that moment in time I was willing to pay *any* price to get there. *Any* price.

And *that,* ladies and gentlemen, is when all hell breaks loose.

Chapter 4

At the time, I was already functioning at church as the singles ministry leader, and it was when I first took that position that I began to understand how God brings to birth what some people call *vision*. I'm not really sure where vision comes from. Perhaps it is in the seeds of vague dissatisfaction, where the longing for something intangible and nameless starts to take form and becomes a dream.

It is birthed in a restlessness that is undefined and it becomes something you find yourself praying for at a stoplight, and when you are weeding the garden, or when you first awaken. You may not even know how to pray for it. You babble a prayer on your first waking, coherent moment that resembles, "I don't know what you want me to do, Lord, but just bring me there and let me recognize it when I see it as being Yours".

Sometimes Vision is accompanied by a mental picture and at that point the pieces start to drop into place of their own volition, like puzzle pieces that know where they are supposed to go. It is something that whispers to you at twilight and keeps you awake at midnight, and the longing for it becomes your companion. Vision, like childbirth, is a painful thing, and your fear of the unknown is counterbalanced by your excitement at what lies ahead, the excitement of bringing forth the child of the whispered promise. And when it is all over and you at last hold the very promise in your arms and embrace it in its reality, you no longer remember the struggle to bring it forth.

When I took on the singles ministry, I'd never actually *been* to a singles ministry meeting before. I didn't even *want* to go to a singles function. I think that I was afraid that I would be dooming myself to that lifestyle if I associated too closely with other singles. I had an erroneous mental picture of desperately lonely people, with little in their life to draw from, who felt that only a relationship would validate them and give them worth and meaning. Some folk are so fixed on this magical solution that *anyone* will do—just plug somebody—anybody—in; and *yet they haven't done the necessary work to make themselves whole so that they have something to contribute to the relationship.* A man or woman with big dreams and an intimate relationship with God is never desperate and needn't be lonely. I didn't trust my mental picture necessarily, which is exactly why I started visiting singles groups. I needed to know what other people were doing and if it was working.

From my visits, I learned that I *still* didn't want to attend a single's group. I know there are singles ministries out there that are very dynamic gatherings, but from the ones I visited, I found that many settle into a couple of predictable patterns. It seemed to me as if everyone had read the same manual on singles groups. In fact, after the singles ministry was going great, someone with good intentions gave me a manual they had picked up on how to do a singles group— and the plan presented in the book was to have the same kind that I was avoiding.

Maybe a lot of the leaders of singles' groups are big on lots of structure— they are people who thrive in a highly structured world. And that's okay if the people who *attend* are very structured people. It makes them feel safe and secure.

But I found that often the scenario went a lot like this. A brown foldout table with rough edges that snag your clothes appeared to be mandatory equipment—along with an overhead projector and bright, intrusive, harsh fluorescent lights. On one side sat some defensive women, their arms crossed and in stony silence. The men sat on the other side or in one corner and they looked really scared of the women. There were a few songs and it seemed as if the only people that knew those songs were the people who attended that particular church. There wasn't a particularly welcoming atmosphere, being held in a classroom or an empty meeting room.

Then there were discussions of things to do like ball games or movies. Then there was a discussion of some scriptures and then everyone went out to eat somewhere. It always seemed as if everyone was waiting for the whole thing to be over with so they could get to the Going-Out-To-Eat-Somewhere part because that is what they really needed. They *wanted* a lack of structure where they could converse in a non-threatening atmosphere. Church services are already structured. So are Bible studies. And prayer meetings. Structure, structure, structure.

Another aspect (this has been substantiated by many other singles who have confided to me their frustrations in their own churches) was that many of the singles ministries out there are led by married couples. Moreover, the married couple has been married so long, i.e. to a high school or college sweetheart, that they have completely lost touch with what it is like to even *be* single. They lead the singles group and then go home to their partner.

Now I realize that in some churches there isn't a single who wants to be the Singles' Leader. They feel like the blind leading the blind. Still, in other churches, a single person is not *permitted* to be the singles ministry leader. That unfortunate fact leaves a big ol' "Why?" in my mind. Maybe it is because the leadership thinks that singles need someone to keep an eye on them? This shouldn't be necessary if the pastor and their spouse occasionally join the singles for discussion and fellowship, and make themselves available to adequately train the prospective leader. I issued invitations to each of the pastors in my church for the opening night of The Open Door Cafe. I wanted them to share what was happening. I wanted to remove any doubt about what was transpiring on a typical Saturday night.

More often than not, however, the problem is that pastors see single people as dysfunctional people with a Trustworthiness Deficit. They see singles as having a lot of baggage, being broken and needing relationships. (I think Jesus referred to them as "the poor in spirit"). Or, the leadership sees them as somehow incomplete—as if only having a partner validates them.. This often drives a compulsion to find a partner in some singles, because they *just want to be included*, rather than *ex*cluded in social gatherings. It also drives the need to be a couple just so you will not be considered abnormal by the people in your own church.

Perhaps the leadership believes the single person in question is too vulnerable to temptation, which is often the unspoken case. Actually, I have yet to find a single person who is cheating on their spouse.

Sometimes, singles are even seen as childlike because they are unmarried. I was told of an instance where the person in question was *thirty years old*, and in a successful career— and when they approached their pastor about initiating a project, was told, "Well, it's a great idea, *but I think that we ought to have one of the adults head that up, don't you think?*"

What?

Marriage does not validate people, nor does it make them mature (some *married* individuals can vouch for that one!).

The point is, if God *gave* them a partner, they *would* be married. Marriage is something God puts together and it is a holy thing. Because He hasn't given someone a partner, they are, in their single state, walking precisely in the will of God for that point in time. There's not "something wrong with them".

Then, there is the very real feeling expressed by many singles of feeling invisible in their own church. There are young married groups, college and career groups, and seniors groups. A church of four or five hundred people often offers nothing in terms of support for singles. A large proportion of church budgets go to youth and children's programs. All of these are worthy of support. However, there are some things many churches overlook.

Usually in churches, singles groups are relegated to whatever room is not being used for youth, despite the fact that the group of single Christians is an ever-*growing* segment of the church populace, which will grow even *larger* as the Baby Boomers lose spouses. No church has the luxury of overlooking this untapped resource.

Single individuals, without children (or even with children) are a Mother Lode of Resources and insight into the very communities the churches are trying to reach. Think of all the singles who are not in churches— that need ministry. Are we to wait until they are actually sitting in the pews before we reach out to them (if *then*)?

Regardless of the single status of the apostle Paul (consider the fact that we Christians today are a result of *his* fruitful ministry), singles are looked upon with a wary eye. I often think that Paul would feel nearly invisible in a church of today, overlooked or perhaps looked upon warily because "there must be something *wrong* with him or he wouldn't be single."

I'm not making this up. Time after time I've heard it from the people who came to my singles group.

So often, I wanted to address churches, and as the bearer of bad news inform those that are married that some day, *fifty percent of them will be single!* Which one of the couple will it be, assuming they don't die together in an accident? Will they end up sitting home alone, week after week, or will there be a community of single adults to offer encouragement and support, a group to draw inspiration from, and a group to serve? Is anyone aware of the dramatic shortening of life span for those who live alone? It's because they are lonely and sad. What if the pastor *himself* was suddenly single, or the pastor's *wife*? What then?

After visiting a few groups I went back to try some ideas. The first idea was a group book reading. Not that we sat and read to each other, but we read the same book; and then on the final Saturday of the month we would meet to discuss what was read. I thought of the wealth of inspiration being imparted by a large group reading the same uplifting work. Attendance?

Two. Including myself.

This lasted for about four agonizing weeks. I considered it the learning curve. The book was really good, and spoke reams to my heart and soul, but it just didn't seem to be the ticket.

What else would work? Let's try.... Group journaling! Yeah, that's it. I bought some three-subject notebooks and the first Saturday I tried it, we had the same two people. The second meeting, there were three people. There was some interesting discussion, but then again, something was drastically wrong.

Meeting after meeting I would sit there facing Leslie, the church secretary and one of the few singles in our church. I barely knew her, but she was there faithfully every final Saturday. The first tenuous nights we shared between the two of us the paths we had taken that brought us to Christ and eventually to this place of single motherhood. We shared openly the mistakes we had made and our heart's desire to become all we were meant to be.

Over the weeks, I learned that she was good at *all* the things I wasn't. Where I was petite with short unmanageable hair and a few freckles, she was tall and slender with dark hair and ... bunches of freckles— and could reach *all* the cabinets in the church kitchen! Where I was forgetful at times, and seemed to accomplish things almost by accident, knowing the broad vision for the task at hand— she was always able to anticipate what I needed, remember what I was about to forget, and have it right there within my grasp in seconds flat. It was *uncanny,* her way of anticipating — it was as if God knew my deficiencies and gave me two extra hands.

She became my partner in prayer and also my friend. She taught me the value of constancy— and became a precious confidante to whom I was accountable. There is thirteen years difference in our ages, but we have always related as if we were the same age. I've never known anyone like her, probably because there just *isn't* anyone like her. She has, through her quiet and humble way taught me more about being a Christian than just about anybody.

Final Saturday after final Saturday we would look at each other, trying so hard to have The-Single's Group, and finally, one Saturday night, we burst out laughing, and pointing a stern finger to each other, solemnly vowed that we would not *"despise the day of small beginnings."* I have often wondered since how the two of us came to be such constant friends, since we were so very different. All we can conclude is that our friendship is a gift of God to encourage and strengthen two single mothers.

One night, I had a hard time falling asleep. The singles' group was floundering and I didn't know how to fix it. I was leading a single's group that *I* didn't even want to attend. It was too hard to think up a different activity each month—as if I was a puppeteer deciding what everyone *else* would think enjoyable. I was trying to give everyone what I thought they wanted, but the trouble with that is, you can't get inside everyone's head and figure that out. I knew I wasn't having much fun, so I couldn't expect others to. As it was, I felt as if I was going through the motions without my own heart being in it.

Looking back on it, I can only think it was because I was trying to be what I thought a single's group leader was *supposed* to be. I think there had been some expectations communicated about how I was supposed to lead it, but none of those expectations took into account my gifts and strengths. It was as if I thought there was a cardboard cutout Ministry Leader that my own likeness and personality had to conform to, and I was supposed to poke my face through the hole and "be that". I was trying to *play the role* of a singles group leader without being who *I* was, without utilizing the gifts I was created with. I was not aware at that time that all of the tools and abilities I would need to do something incredible were created in me and were just waiting for the right format to find expression. I would never have been good at doing all the things those other people were doing because I wasn't them.

I was good at being me, and that is all God needed. In fact, I had already been using every talent I needed at my former employer.

As I lay there staring at the leaf pattern cast on the wall by the streetlight, I thought out the problem.

First of all, every singles group I knew of met once a month (or less), always on the first ____-day, or the last ____-day.

The only trouble is, singles are single *all month long.* Meeting once a month just doesn't cut it. It just isn't enough to really help people connect and make friendships with people who share the same boat-not to mention the fact that there is no physical contact with another human soul, sometimes for months.

Hold *it*! I know what you're thinking. Physical *con*tact? As in ... *Touching*?

Absolutely. If you're married reading this, you know how important a hug or a pat on the arm can be. Imagine going a week— or three— without anyone patting you on the back, a friendly push, or a heartfelt hug. Imagine no one ever reaching out to you and laying a comforting hand on your arm, even though you may be going through incredible trials— especially as a single parent, or a single parent with a chronically ill child.

That is exactly what it is like for so many who live alone, or even single parents. What if your child never had anyone hold and comfort them? There have been studies done on infants in orphanages where there was very little physical contact, and many die for lack of touch, mysteriously termed "failure to thrive".

Then I started thinking of what I would find fun to do. After all, if *I* couldn't get excited about it, how could I expect anyone else to? So often it seems that we should evaluate how we are perceived by others by how we would respond if we were the other person. In other words, would *we* want to spend time around *us*. Would I be bored by me? It was always my motto that when I gave a gift, it should be something that I myself would love to have.

I began by asking myself what my fondest memories were, what were some of my own cheap thrills? I thought of going to the restaurants that I had frequented while a college student at the University of Cincinnati. They were the kind of places where your Earth Shoes made a comforting sound on the wooden floors and incense hung in the air above the slice of raspberry fudge cake.

I had spent hours sitting at the kitchen table talking with my mom during college about the coffee house/*Patisserie* I would have if I ruled the world. I planned with her the menu, and the decorating- as if I could already see it. I was twenty at the time.

Then the most amazing thing happened.

I thought, *"Lord, what if I could re-create that at the church?"* Immediately, a mental picture of how it would look flashed across my closed eyelids, along with the thought, *"Well, Lord, it's gotta have a name, You know."*

Immediately it came to me— The Open Door Café!

In fact, I tried to think up other names for it but nothing really seemed to fit. It was a name that settled into place like the last puzzle piece or the sound of an old metal Band-Aid box clicking shut. Most of all, it reminded me that *He is always at the door*, waiting for us to invite Him into our lives. I felt that my door should always be open, a lot like my heart.

Let me tell you, if I couldn't sleep for the problem, it was even *worse* when I discovered the solution! My imagination took off in one glorious and unbridled direction, and it flowed effortlessly. I felt like a little kid who can't wait for the first day of summer vacation.

I could take a classroom at the church and turn it into a living room, if you will, and then change it back for Sunday morning services and Sunday school! It would only involve a few props and some of the furniture I could leave there, in little storage areas. I would have little tables and candles and it would look really cool. I approached my pastor with my idea, and he gave me the go ahead to use a room that was serving as a preschool Sunday school class.

Let me just stop right here and say a word about pastors. You will never be so blessed as when you have a pastor who is also a man of vision and is secure enough in himself that he doesn't feel threatened by the dreams and visionary, entrepreneurial endeavors of those he shepherds. He is secure enough in himself that he doesn't have to feel as if he's in absolute control of everything— but instead believes in your God-breathed abilities. After all, the object is to pastor a flock in which you fully develop your people to walk in the anointing of their gifts and talents.

I painted the room and on the first Saturday of *many* Saturdays, I went over to the church at three in the afternoon and prepared everything.

The room setting itself involved moving a short but *very* heavy toddler table out of the room. I wrestled with it until I got it on its side and then *rolled* it out of the room, wondering, *"What in the world is this thing made of—concrete?"* It was for people only 30 inches high, but would have been perfectly at home in a WWII bunker! I "walked" a heavy file cabinet out of the room and stacked what seemed like three hundred seventeen gnome-sized chairs on the other side of some concealing draperies. I wedged a wing chair into the trunk of my '95 Subaru, and likewise hauled various one-of-a-kind accessories to the church. Drapes were then hung at the window and across the opening of the adjoining room/gnome-chair storage room. I brought a table lamp and a Queen Ann end table, added two rocking chairs and three card tables covered with tablecloths, small lamps and flowers. With the addition of candles and some framed pictures the room was ready. It was genuinely cozy and inviting.

Then I set about preparing the food. Sometimes Leslie was able to help when her schedule was free. It was great fun—you really can't beat the combination of two women in a kitchen with a Big Idea.

The workout started early the next morning when I headed back over to the church at five-thirty and undid everything, hanging Jesus and the disciples back on the wall along with Noah and five dozen cutouts of hands, that changed to pumpkins and then to snowflakes as the year progressed.

And so for a year and a half I went to the church on Saturday afternoon to transform the classroom into The Open Door Café. Then back again early the next morning to change it back again. I was beginning to wish that there was a secret button, which would turn bookcases and walls around to make an entirely different room like in old movies of castles with secret passages. I had become a master at spatial relationships, knowing just how much furniture and accessories could fit into a Subaru sedan (you'd be amazed). I could have used two or three of me.

Now, it would be a Serious Mistake to think that what I've been writing about in this chapter/book is about singles ministry. It's not about a Singles Ministry, and it isn't even about me! It's about you.

While the subject I've addressed is how I operated a really good singles group by a lot of trial and error, it is *really* about ordinary but courageous individuals overcoming public opinion, their fears, their circumstances and their limited imagination to make their dreams come true. Your dreams can't really come true unless you get one, either. I am only showing you how I did what I did, what my thought process was, and how I made mistakes on my way to success. I believe everyone reading this has a dream, a destiny—something you believe you are "Supposed to Do". I'm here to tell you something vitally important:

There is *absolutely nothing* stopping you from doing the thing you have always dreamt of doing, with the possible exception of two words that you should *never*— EVER — allow to enter your mind or escape your lips: *"I can't"*.

Chapter 5

Despite the fact that I had a wonderful beginning to my ministry, I still very much needed to support my family. Naturally, in a situation like being downsized, you start to look at your own abilities, your resources. If, as the scriptures say, God works in us to not only will, but also *do* His good pleasure, then it only follows that, if we are walking with Him and dwelling in His presence, He will place desires in our heart which align with His desires for our life, and also give us the tools and resources with which to accomplish those desires.

To take it a step further, let me propose that you *already* have in your hands or at least somewhere at your disposal, everything you need to accomplish something truly remarkable. If you were to get off by yourself and clear your head, I'd also be willing to bet that there is a desire buried deep in you heart. Maybe your dream has lingered there for so long you've almost forgotten you even had a dream once. And to add even more excitement, I would even go so far as to say that the desire you have probably matches up with the tools you either already have or have access to.

So what did I have at hand? I looked at the training and experience I had had some years before with children with developmental challenges—and I had been seeking information from various people with Children's Services. I was thinking that I would do childcare in my home for children who had slight disabilities—children who simply needed one-on-one attention. I had worked as a volunteer several years earlier with a program that helped to identify, through diagnostic testing of incoming kindergarten children, those who were at a slight disadvantage in skills that would help them succeed in school. Through working closely to practice small and large motor skills, visual acuity, etc. we brought them up to a more competitive level with other children their age. All of this seemed to be a viable solution. And so off I mentally ran with the idea of starting a day care/tutoring program in my home for challenged children...

Pardon me, but did I *forget* to mention that my home was filled to the brim with antiques, Queen Anne (I wonder if her legs ever *really* looked like that?) and rare Irish china? In no time at all, I went to work like a Trojan. After all, I was... On-n a-a-ah- Mission-n-n-n.

I emptied my garage of gardening implements and tools and turned it into a large muscle room, complete with climbing ropes, a balancing beam and hopscotch painted on the floor. From yard sales, I found baby toys and games, a toy train set and (I'm estimating) one thousand seventy-three (I'm kidding-it was really two thousand) large cardboard building blocks. I painted an aerial scene on the floor that you could play with little cars and trains on, and outside I painted white shutters on the otherwise pink garage. I took the porch swing off the front porch and suspended it from the beams in the newly constructed playroom. I had colorful banners hanging from the walls and all in all, it was quite bright and cheery—despite the fact it started off with two dead birds in it and part of a dead squirrel, the unfortunate dinner guests for a white stray cat I thought of naming Hannibal.

It had been transformed from singularly grisly to simply charming.

I had a representative come out from Children's Services and she liked what I had done to prepare for the little ones I would care for. But after our visit I learned some unsettling news that wasn't disclosed on my initial contacts with them. There was a limit to the number of children you could have per childcare worker, and on a sliding scale, there is no way I would be paid adequately enough. There really wasn't any way that going through their agency would work. It would have been great as a second income, say, if I had been married, but not at all if you were Plan A *and* Plan B.

But even without the umbrella of Children's Services, it seemed to be doomed before I started. Although I publicized it all over, hardly anyone seemed to call. And if they did, they never kept the appointment. It was such an uncanny thing. People would make appointments to come by and meet, *but they never showed up.* And it got worse! Day after day it was the same thing.

I'd heard of things like this happening before.

Was this Isaac on the altar, was this yet another instance when, at the last moment, God would show up like a Celestial Superhero and pull this out of the fire? Hey, I had all the verses on my refrigerator too. Any day now I would have a miracle.

Yessiree… any day now.

Then, a really awful thought occurred to me and it gnawed at my ankles, pulled at my sleeve until I gave it me undivided attention.

What if I was wrong? What if I hadn't heard Him at all? The Shadow Talk started. You've heard shadow talk before. It's the voice of self-doubt and self-condemnation. It is the voice of Shouldas and Couldas.

God and I had a meeting. No, actually we had a lot of meetings. It eventually turned into The Meeting That Would Not Die. The only problem was, He didn't say much. I talked to a few other people and asked their advice. I considered just chucking the whole thing and getting a job, but I wondered if that would mean I had given up on the verge of a breakthrough. What would He say face to face when we discuss this little chapter in The Life of Caron? Was He to tell me how disappointed He was that I gave up so easily? Was my strength that small? How do we know when to give up? Or *do* we give up? Did I misinterpret what He'd said in the first place? Was I only hearing *myself*? What happens when this happens?

I was on the edge of a miracle, all right. But I was all wrong about the miracle. I have learned that sometimes we have to let God choose the miracles. We have to let Him be sovereign— in even the smallest of things. It hurts, especially when we are going full steam ahead and He wants us to make a sharp left or worse—reverse.

Many times He asks us to be the opposite of who we have always been. He takes Deep Thinkers and gives them the simple stuff to contemplate. Sometimes He allows us to be captured by a vision. I soon found that I was immersed in a vision of such possibility, such promise, and so simply obvious that I might as well have tripped over it. It was the sort of unorthodox and novel idea that could only be from the mind of God.

Wasn't it poetic that I had always said, "Inside the body of this extrovert, there is an introvert screaming to get in"? Now I found myself embarking on an idea that would be the stretching of me. Wasn't it just like God to take the man who stuttered and make him a public speaker— a leader of thousands in a desert on the other side of East Nowhere, to make a shepherd boy a warrior and king?

Up to that point of my life, it had always been The Caron Show, with an occasional guest appearance by the Lord of Hosts.

Okay, once or twice He had been the co-star.

I didn't consciously do it, it just never really occurred to me that He would be interested in using me to do anything of any consequence.. But through a sequence of difficult and tragic events, there seemed to be increasingly less room for me, and proportionately more room for Him.

And so I would be the latest in the long line of most unlikely servants of the Lord whose qualifications didn't seem at all to be what the job demanded. I submit to you that you already have the desire, the tools and the talent to bring about incredible good for others at this very moment.

Chapter 6

It was during this unsettled time I became concerned with the future of The Open Door Café. Taking a look at the lack of room and the fact that our church was undergoing construction that took away the space I was using for the cafe, it seemed the coffee house was doomed.

During that time, I mentioned to someone at a get-together that the Children's Services thing didn't work out and that I really didn't know quite what to do.

"What do you really *want* to do?" she queried.

"I want to have The Open Door Cafe in my home." The words jumped out from a place I didn't know existed— somewhere close to my heart, I think— and the answer took me by surprise. It was as if the words and the desire had been held back by a flood-gate, waiting for the question to be asked.

"Really?" she mused, her eyebrows raised. "How would you go about that?"

I muttered something about giving it some thought and didn't say much more about it. Inside, however, it was another story. It's all I could think about and the weird thing was, it would only involve a couple of very minor adjustments. It was as if I was looking at the whole thing all along, and yet not seeing it—like those pictures at the mall that look like speckles of color until your eye relaxes and suddenly you're looking at dolphins beneath the sea.

I should also mention that just a few days before this, I had been thinking about going to hear the blues played at an area nightspot.

The only trouble is, though I really like blues and jazz, I didn't want to compromise my Christian testimony and character by going, as a single woman, to what would be considered a nightclub. I just kind of felt that I would be inviting something I wouldn't want into my life. I was contemplating this sitting on the loveseat in my living room, when I said to myself, almost out loud, "You know, Lord, what this town needs is a gathering place where you could reasonably be assured of meeting up with other Christians, and not worry about compromising. The only trouble is, I can't afford any real estate.

How could I manage to do it without having to pay for a separate site?"

I thought about how I would want it to look, and then concluded that it should look very much like a house. It should be cozy and relaxing. In the back of my mind, I was thinking it could look like my house. How odd it seemed that my acquaintance would ask me just a few days later what I really wanted to do, and I responded almost without thinking that I wanted to have a home café.

The next day was Monday. I sat down and planned out what I would have to do to get it ready to host The Open Door Café in my home.

First, I would have to go from holding the café on the final Saturday of the month to every week.

Woah! Every *week*?

I really hadn't wanted to make that commitment in the past. After all, what if *I* wanted to do something on a whole weekend, like taking my daughters camping or, well— *something*. Okay, it wasn't like I was *that* busy. I just wanted to reserve my entire weekend so that I could indulge my own preferences. Suddenly, my own preferences didn't seem to matter any more. I realized that Potential for Doing Good was light years beyond the selfish desire to indulge my freedom for Just in Cases. More accurately, there was nothing that I wanted to do on a weekend *more* than I wanted to host the café every weekend. It was just a simple shift in priorities.

Suddenly, by using the gifts and resources I already had, the café became, well, possible, first of all, and secondly, *fun*. I was to finally have the freedom to use my gifts to benefit other people. It wasn't for an employer, or for anyone else, other than the direct beneficiaries of my actions. I imagined all the people who had a hard week at work, all the people who came home to an empty house where there was once laughter. They would come to my house on Saturday nights and engage in lively conversation, eat delicious food and drink coffee. I imagined them sharing their lives and making new friends. They would have something to look forward to all week!

Second, I would need the entire downstairs. Now, it just happened that my bedroom was in what was originally a study— there were only two bedrooms upstairs, and the bathroom. So I decided to take down my four-poster bed and put it out in the garage. I could move the loveseat into the study and sleep there, since I was only five feet tall. I could crunch up on a loveseat. No problem.

I filled the inoperable fireplace with candles and rearranged the layout to accommodate extra people. I bought an extra table at a yard sale and sanded it down so it was useable.

Then I took an inventory of what I would need to host the café on a typical Saturday night. I would need... wait just a minute — I already *had* all the china and silverware I *needed*, every chair and every napkin. I had little restaurant-style lamps for every corner and every table. It was all stuff I had been schlepping around for the last four years, thinking, "This is too good to just give away. Surely if God gave me all this stuff, maybe He wants me to do something with it."

All of it was what I had inherited from my parents, particularly my mother who had every kitchen power-tool known to man and at least five complete sets of dishes in her basement. She had all kinds of specialty baking pans, table linens, and vases.

If I learned resourcefulness and ingenuity from my father, from my mother I learned the gracious trait of walking in abundance. The point is, there was a lot of lovely furniture I simply gave away to people who had a need— whole rooms full of furniture because I had way more than my house would accommodate— and I still had a bunch of stuff! Some things, however, I kept for— well, I didn't even know *what* at the time; it just seemed like it would be useful for something—such as a catering business or, well, *this very project*.

Though I could not see it at the time (which was about three years earlier), all of these things had a theme, and they had The Open Door Café written all over them.

Now, stop right here and think back over your life. Is there a common thread that runs through your life, a dream or desire? Do you have— or could you easily get— the tools you need to accomplish your dream? Do you see how God has supplied you with the means to do something really remarkable that would be a blessing to a *lot of other people?*

So, what's stopping you? Is there a hurdle that is self-inflicted, that, if you really thought about it, isn't *really* an obstacle to your dream? Many of the things we see as obstacles are not really insurmountable at all. It is only our thinking that makes it appear to be an obstacle. If you can't get in the door, you gotta go in through the window.

It's all in your head. I always say, "It's all mind over matter—if you don't mind, it just doesn't matter!"

Chapter 7

October. It is the best of months. I wanted the café to open at my home in October because autumn has always seemed to be a gathering-in time. Gathering of harvest, gathering in of our summer ramblings, gathering of family and dear friends. The chilly days make you long for the closeness and laughter of your children and the merriment of long time companions. Now, I realize that the coming of fall and winter brings some folks down. But it needn't. That is when you light more candles, call up a friend, and play more music. Take up a hobby, or an instrument.

I spent the day polishing, dusting, vacuuming, scouring and otherwise consecrating my home. I also painted a sign for the front porch so that I could hang it on a little nail. I had an old plant light that sat on a base or you could hang it on a wall, which I used as a makeshift spotlight. The sign was Real Cute.

I also fasted that day, praying for those who would be my guests. In fact, fasting on the day of the café became part of the preparations, it was an act of worship, as was the washing of the dishes, and the cooking and the brewing of the coffee. There was hardly a Saturday that I didn't fast and pray for everyone who would walk through my door that night. They probably never knew that until they see it on this page.

"Lord, just bring the people who should be here *this* night. I don't care about the numbers— I'll be just as happy if there is one person as twenty."

It was getting toward evening and things were just about ready. I hoped I wouldn't have to turn on the air conditioner because I wanted the natural autumn air to accentuate the feeling of being gathered in to the hearth— the heart— of my home. Isolated crickets chirped and the scent of leaves on the turn of autumn hung in the air. I finished washing a cream pitcher and dried my hands. I then I lit a candle and placed it on the windowsill of the small paned window above the kitchen sink. Soon it would be dark outside. I stood there, watching the small flame sway back and forth. The reflection and shadows cast on a small white pitcher near the candle was mesmerizing. My heart was full that night, as it would be for the years to follow: full of anticipation, full of the glow of friends *I was yet to make* (I swear, I loved them already), and most of all, full of wonder and *Mystery*. I was embarking on a journey, a Real Life Adventure of my own making.

It was as if I had set off, far from my safe Hobbit house, provisions for the journey ahead tucked into my sack. Only the journey before me was one of giving without thought of getting, opening my heart to really know and love others— even if they were difficult. *Anything could happen.* I was so keenly aware of the possibilities which were mathematically infinite, as I stood there at the sink, knowing that whatever was going to happen was big. Really big.

The discovery I would make was of myself, for my desire also defined my identity. Long since I hosted the cafe people have said to me, "Caron, you're still you, even if you don't have a coffee house." On one level that is true, but perhaps they have never themselves discovered the immense joy of that glimpse of heaven, the *knowledge that at a certain point in time, you are doing what you were always meant to do.*

I wanted the atmosphere in my home to be extraordinary, and it was. I wanted people to know they had been somewhere magical and like none other when they came to The Open Door Café.

The coffee was already brewed and the aroma filled the entire downstairs. I made two homemade pies and a fruit tray, which I placed on a great sideboard in the living room. Above the sideboard was a huge gold-framed mirror and I had cut some fresh flowers from the yard—the last of my garden flowers for a while. I lit bunches of candles, placing them in every room and put on some music—it was

Irish, of course. The whole house was furnished in antiques—things that had been in my family since I was little. There was an oval picture of my grandmother at ten years of age, in 1915, with her high button shoes and black hair. There were candles a-plenty in the fireplace, which featured a large carved mantle incorporating a mirror. Oriental carpets stretched the expanse of the dark, fondly worn hardwood floors and spread a pattern in salmon, then gold and then gray-blue from room to room to room. You could make your way from the foyer to the living room, to the dining room and kitchen and back again to the foyer, and every room carried a feeling all it's own.

After hurrying through a shower, applying makeup, and hastily finger-arranging my contrary hair, I put on a black dress (black is universally versatile, and you can dress it up or down), pearl earrings, and dashed downstairs. I made myself busy in the kitchen, wiping the silver serving pieces, arranging little cookies on a plate.

And then I waited.

Finally the front doorbell rang.

"There's actually a guest! What do I do now?"

I was so taken aback, I suddenly felt flustered and smoothing my dress hurried in to the front door, completely forgetting my shoes. I opened it to an older gentleman who stepped inside and offered his hand. His name was Vince. I had seen him once before at one of the single's functions I'd attended, and had him sign my guest book on a little Queen Anne table in the front hallway. He then made his way into the living room and took a seat. I offered him a cup of coffee and asked him how he took it. He drank coffee with me for a while and said very little, despite my polite questions. The grandfather clock ticked in the background, keeping time with a fiddle from the stereo. After about an hour, he got up and said goodnight, then I walked him to the front door. That night Vince was the only guest of The Open Door Café.

My daughters and my son who came to visit *loved* the pies I had made for the guests that never came.

The next week, I did what I had done the week before. Only it was a *schnechen* tea ring — a German coffeecake that my mother always made for special occasions— that and a cheese and cracker tray, along with veggies and dip and hot finger foods artfully arranged on the sideboard. Again there were candles and the music was Dave Brubeck along with Henry Mancini, Stan Getz, and all that jazz

Vince was once again my solitary guest, and he drank, once again, a single cup of coffee as we made pleasant conversation. He didn't seem to mind that there wasn't anyone else there. He politely said goodnight, thanking me for the conversation and I closed the door.

I stood there for a moment, with my back leaning against the door, my thoughts hovering between uncertainty and faith, when I was startled by the doorbell again. It was Ellen, the one to whom I had confided my desire to have the café in my home. She asked if anyone else had been there. I told her only Vince, my guest from the week before. But I added that I would not "despise the day of small beginnings", thinking back to Leslie and myself trying to be The Single's ministry. Ellen and I prayed for the weeks that would follow. We prayed for God to show up. Afterwards we hugged and she left. I closed the front door behind her and turned off the porch light. I decided I would keep on keeping on.

During the following week, I kept praying for the people who would walk through the door of the Open Door Café, not just for the next Saturday, but for ever. I prayed that God would meet their needs in every area— that they would sense His presence in my home. I prayed that they would be touched by the kindness shown by a total and complete stranger. That God would make me into the person who would make them feel welcome. I didn't know that He already had done all of those things.

The next Saturday, the third week in October, it had turned colder. There were no crickets to be heard outside the kitchen window in the twilight and the darkness came on sooner. I lit a candle and placed it in the little window above the sink, which still had the rustic wooden screen in it and the light from that flame warmed my soul. I remembered I had done the same thing the first night of The Open Door Cafe, and now I was headed into week three. I stared at it a bit, knowing in my heart that I was on the edge of something that would be life changing; yet I didn't know what it was.

I baked blueberry muffins and banana bread as desserts and that afternoon. I made a spinach and broccoli quiche. Piecrust was always a specialty of my mother's and it had become mine. I prayed for the people who would eat each muffin, and as I placed each cup on the sideboard, I prayed for each of the people who would drink from the cups.

On the stove was a big stockpot of hot mulled apple cider, which sent the most delicious aroma up the stairs and coaxed my daughters, one after another of them down the stairs.

"I hope nobody comes to your dumb coffee house, Mom." quipped Abby, as she ladled a cup of cider from the stove.

Suddenly the front door bell (literally a bell on a rivet, which allowed it to swing when tipped by hand) rang and before I could open it, the front door opened and three strangers, a man and two women stepped inside the door.

"Is this the café?" asked one of the women. "I wasn't expecting it to be in, you know, a *house*."

"It sure is!" I returned, trying desperately to contain my unbridled excitement. "Please— come in! Here, just put your jackets here on this post—that's what we always do."

"I feel like I'm at home!" she said, draping her coat over the newel post. "Oh, it smells so good in here, doesn't it Bob?"

"Hey, I hope that's for us." Bob joked, nodding toward the buffet. We made introductions all around, and everyone seemed not only to be grateful for finding the place, but finding it to be warm and hospitable. I led them in to where the coffee was— and to the buffet.

"The entire downstairs is open to coffee house guests, but I have to insist that you stay downstairs. The upstairs is completely off-limits. It's the only way my kids will let me do this!" I laughed as I followed them into the living room. I already felt I had made new friends.

The doorbell rang again. It almost startled me, and from the corner of my eye I saw the girls quietly take off for their bedrooms—before any more "Old People" invaded their territory.

I opened the door and it was another group who had driven all the way from Connersville, Indiana in a van to get there — three women and two men who had a singles ministry going in their little town.

And finally there was Vince, who started it all by being faithfully present each of the preceding Saturday nights. We spent the night in lively conversation, and I made three pots of coffee before it was all over.

At length, the Connersville caravan decided it was time to leave as they had to drive over an hour to get home, but they promised they would come again. I hugged the last visitor and held open the wooden screen door before them as they made their way out onto the porch, down the steps, and to their cars. They were calling good wishes and goodnights all the way. They had had a good time, and that meant the world to me.

The air was chilly now. I was tired, but felt incredibly peaceful and *filled up*. There were nine people that night that built a sense of community with total strangers. They knew that, come what may —or may not, there was always a place for them on a Saturday night when the only other option was an empty house.

I turned off the porch light as the last of my new friends pulled away.

The next week would bring the time change, the colors of autumn, and the most unexpected surprise! But in addition to the surprise, there was the foreshadowing of something full of menace. There will almost always be opposition to any bold and miraculous endeavor, and the threat is almost always in proportion to the good to be done. Trouble was brewing right along with the coffee at the Open Door Cafe, and it coincided with the first night I ever opened my door.

Chapter 8

I had occasionally visited a Christian Single's web site that was part of a national magazine's site, as it featured articles written by singles regarding the life and challenges faced by single Christians. Toward the end of October of 1999, a new columnist was to debut on the site. I read her first article and was moved to write to her to thank her for her transparency about her own single life, and to encourage her.

Then I told her not to be discouraged about her single lifestyle and that I was a single mother and that I ran a Christian Singles coffeehouse from my home.

The next day, I came home from work and checked my email while I waited for the pasta to boil. There was a note in my mailbox from the columnist I had written to encourage. I hadn't even expected a reply—I guess I thought all the letters would go into a black hole or something. She wrote back and said, "When I told the other staff writers of *Today's Christian Woman* about your café, they said they would like to do a feature article for the magazine".

Stop the presses.

What's she *saying* here? I printed it off took it into Maureen's room where the girls were watching *Stand By Me*. Someone on the movie was saying "*LOO*-NY!", appropriately enough.

"Hey, girls, would someone read this and tell me what it says."

I just didn't trust me.

Maureen paused the movie, and taking the page with the ink still damp, scanned it briefly before handing it back and turning her attention back to the movie. "It looks like they want to do an article about your dumb coffeehouse, mom."

Kids know just how to inspire you, don't they? I remembered how tough it was to negotiate with them a way to do the café from our house— they made me *promise* that no Old People would come upstairs and it could *only* be on Saturday nights.

After a while, though, they came to love Saturday nights as much as my guests and I did, and they readily helped in the preparations. Eventually, they would come downstairs and get plates of quiche and hors d'ouevres and talk with some of the guests, though since the girls were shy, it was usually the guests who initiated the conversation.

I was so very surprised by the recent development. I exchanged some emails concerning the details of how it would all come together, and it was decided that on December 22nd they would come to do the photo shoot. I kept expecting to find out it had all been a big misunderstanding. If it was all true, what on earth did it mean? Was it just an isolated "happy accident", as I like to name such occurrences, or was it a passport to something else that was yet to come? Would it bring in a lot more people to the cafe, or was it to simply meant to encourage me that I was truly on the right path—and not just, well, loony?

I had come to observe and anticipate "coincidences" on a regular basis, the strength of which I measured by the relative (im)probablility of such an occurrence. In other words, the more far-out the coincidence, the greater the meaning *behind* it.

Finally, as the evening approached, and I gave the photographer directions to my house from Indianapolis (there was a solitary right turn, once you got off I-75) it began to take on The Cloak of Reality.

The house was decked-out for Christmas, as it had been since the antique horse-drawn carriage and sled parade three weeks before. In fact, most of the houses in Lebanon are very dressed up for the holiday, and this is never more true than of the Victorian homes, which just naturally lend themselves to Christmas—"Dickensed-out" as I call it.

I was expecting more people that week since it was during Christmas, so I made extra desserts. The buffet was laden with all sorts of delicious finger foods and desserts. There were three dozen candles lit and placed throughout the rooms and their wonderful aroma filled the house— why, it smelled as if I'd been baking for hours (which was quite true). Everywhere you looked it was absolutely Christmas.

Surprisingly, however, when the photographer and his assistant arrived, they had to take down all the Christmas decorations in the room where they would be taking the photos, as the article was to appear in the April-May issue. They were very apologetic, and we even had fun un-decorating, while I pretended to be miffed. They tested the lights all different ways so that the atmosphere could be duplicated, even going so far as to simulate the evening light of early spring coming through the window in the background.

Guests started arriving by the time they were ready to take the pictures, so I corralled them in the foyer. There was a lot of frivolity going on in the other room, and some kept pretending to try to sneak hors d'oeuvres from the buffet to make me laugh.

Being a shy person, I never really liked being in photographs, I liked taking them. Some eight hundred thirty-five snapshots later (it only seemed like that many) they packed it all in. What had taken hours to prepare took only a few moments to put away, and soon the photographer and his assistant were sipping coffee and sampling dessert with the rest of the guests of The Open Door Café.

They were most pleasant, and all of us wished they could stay longer. They had a two hour drive ahead of them, though, back to Indianapolis, so amidst farewells and "Be carefuls" they loaded their car with their equipment and headed back home.

One Sunday four months later, one of the single ladies who came to the coffeehouse frequently (her name was Sandy, but many people called her "The Game Lady" because she always brought a tote bag full of games) sat down in front of me. I was staring at the back of the pew, rather lost in thought, when she turned around and handed a folded magazine to me. I took it from her and glanced down— it was myself I was looking at, holding my own coffee cup, with my own pictures and lamps and candlesticks in the background!

I don't know why I did, but I cried. I needed to know so desperately that what I was doing really mattered— and that I was really on the right path. I had spent so very much time pursuing my own ideas and my own agenda that once sick and tired of it, I wanted more than anything to know I was doing something selfless. I needed to know that there was something eternal being done by my hands, and with all my heart. In addition to being a tremendously humbling experience, it gave me the affirmation that I desperately needed that I really *was* walking in my gifts and calling and that God had His own plan for everyone who called the café home on a Saturday night.

Chapter 9

As I mentioned earlier, the café was being stalked by a dark harbinger of doom.

The previous summer, before I had decided to move the café home and was investigating the Children's Services venture, I'd planned on using some savings in the form of 401K funds from the dealership and from another former employer until I got my venture started. An unexpected repair to the air conditioner swallowed one of the 401Ks whole (I have children with asthma, so air conditioning wasn't an option).

No sooner did I get the air conditioner fixed, but the 28 year-old olive green refrigerator lent to me by a friend expired. I walked into the dark kitchen one morning and saw the refrigerator standing in a pool of rust red liquid. The only thing missing was a square chalk outline on the floor and yellow barrier tape!

I had to replace it. (I tried for a while to convince my children that it would be fun to live like an honest to goodness family from the last century, but they just didn't buy it—refrigeration is a must in this century). It wasn't a problem, as I had another retirement account.

I called the investment counselor's office and spoke to a secretary about liquidating the remaining 401K. It would be enough to more than cover the arrearage in the house payments that were going into acceleration. The timing would be close, but with the amount I had in the account, I would still be able to catch up. The secretary acted very distant and preoccupied. She said that it would take 6 to

8 weeks to receive the check. It would be close, but it would work. I began to look for another job. Not that I wanted to ditch God, but I *was* beginning to panic.

At ten weeks, I hadn't received any word, so I called Dave's office back and he answered the phone. I explained what the secretary had said and that I hadn't heard anything. He replied that he didn't know what had happened, but that the secretary to whom I'd spoken had, at the time, received word that her husband was diagnosed with a brain tumor. He was answering the phone for her because the funeral of her husband was that day. He told me he would call me back in five minutes.

I felt terrible, and I don't know how I would have managed if I had been in her shoes.

True to his word, he called back a few minutes later. The paperwork had never been filed— it was under a stack of papers on her credenza! He said he would do what he could to get me a check by the end of the week. And at five-thirty on Friday afternoon I went down to pick up my check from the dealership. I would call the mortgage company on Monday morning during business hours.

The next morning, Saturday (which, coincidentally, was the first meeting of The Open Door Café) I received the foreclosure notice in the mail.

Monday morning I called them to explain what had happened and they referred me immediately to the legal department. Every time I called thereafter I was forwarded to the legal department. They told me they would not accept my check.

I did not know who to talk to or even what to say. I couldn't tell the girls. I woke up at every conceivable early morning hour with a sick dread (when I *could* sleep), agonizing over what to do. People I did talk to about it kept telling me, "Just call them, they'll work with you. That happened to us and they let us work something out." They evidently didn't have *my* mortgage company.

I had just gotten a job for a local pest control company, but it wasn't nearly enough. Now it was closing in on Christmas. Night after night I prayed for a miracle. I prayed so often during the day that it became a prayer that seemed constant. There was little work to be found at that time of year, and what was available didn't pay adequately.

I suppose I could have worked two jobs, but I had children at home and they needed a parent that was *present*. In a single parent household this is even more pronounced. I felt I had to choose being a parent that was present and available, even if it meant the worst financially. When I sold cars, I realized that there was plenty of money to be made in any type of sales, but the sacrifice would be the long hours I would spend away from my family. Evenings when I was supposed to be off work at six (and had an evening planned with my family or at my daughter's band concert) would come to a screeching halt if a customer, who *could* have made an appointment, walked in the door at five forty-five. There were times when that very thing happened and there were no sales people available to take my customer. So, I was forced to trade closing a sale over attending my daughter's concert.

No amount of money will ever get back for you what is priceless. I look at their pictures of when they were younger, and I would give anything to have them little again. I think to myself, where did the years go? Imagine the regret I would have if I had traded those years away for more cars "out the door".

I know there are folk who will justify making extra money to provide the extra stuff. But when it comes down to it, I think it is more important to "be there" than to have more materially. If we didn't have to have all the toys, then we wouldn't have garages and basements full of stuff we don't use Think of it. Probably most of us need to have a garage sale. We're all buying plastic containers to put our stuff in, and we're all mentally managing all that stuff in our subconscious. What if we just gave it away and uncluttered our garages, basements and subconscious?

I know, it's a scary thought.

I went to work for a temporary agency, but again, since it was the end of the year, many companies weren't even considering hiring until the beginning of the New Year. The job assignments were very few and far between.

One night, my youngest, Emmy — who was then nine, came and sat down next to me on the loveseat in the living room. I had a solitary candle burning on the coffee table and I was drinking a cup of coffee. She sat there quietly and I pulled the cozy blanket up over both of us.

There was a quiet space when we both sat and mused without speaking. Finally Emmy broke the silence.

"Can we put Christmas lights up, mom?"

"Tonight?" I looked at her wincing. "I don't know... it's pretty cold out there for a little girl."

"I can put my coat on— and my hood." She looked up adoringly at me. Her hair was in little braids, and stray curls had crept out of the braids and framed her forehead.

Mothers and fathers live for moments such as these.

"Okay. I think it will make all of us feel more like Christmas, don't you think so? It'll be fun, you'll see!"

Her eyes lit up and a smile flashed across her face as she started crawling out from under the blanket.

I had already gotten the lights out the day before and they were in a box in the hallway. I brought the ladder from the basement landing and we went outside. I had a scarf around my neck, but since I had a hooded sweatshirt under my coat, I took the scarf off and wrapped it around her neck. She was warm as could be, all wrapped up, and a very diligent Christmas-Light Helper. I held the end of the lights and climbed the stepladder while Emmy held the twist ties I always used. I tied the icicle lights, which I had doubled up to twice their density, onto the gingerbread beaded trim of the porch and Emmy unrolled the lights as I made my way around the perimeter.

We were almost done when the headlights of a car shone in my face, and I saw that a police cruiser was pulling over in front of our house. I had no idea what he wanted.

"Emmy, could you do mommy a favor? I need the long white extension cord from the plastic bag under the kitchen sink. Get the really *long* one. Would you do that?"

She nodded and didn't hesitate a bit, but went running inside to look for it. She was, after all, the *only* kid helping with the Very Important Task of hanging the lights.

The wind was bitterly cold and relentlessly bullied its way around the corner of the house. I turned to see a tall husky officer coming up the steps.

"May I help you?" I asked, not really sure of the answer I would get.

"I'm with the Warren County Sheriff's Department. Are you..." he was reading from the paper he held in his gloved hand. — "Car-on Ward?"

"Yes."

Okay, what else *would* I say?

"I'm here to give you these."

I took the papers and in the light of the porch light I could read the top lines—they were from the mortgage company. I looked up and he was already walking down the steps to his car. Didn't he want to *talk* about this a little? Maybe have a cup of coffee? After all, it was awfully cold. And almost Christmas.

Suddenly I felt sorry for him—having to go out on a night like this and give bad news to people. He seemed like such a lonely soul. Emmy came out the front door proudly carrying (and dragging) the long white extension cord.

"Sir?" I called after him. He was almost to the gate of the arbor. He turned around impatiently.

"I know you don't have anything to do with this. Have a Merry Christmas, okay?"

"Yes, ma'am" he touched the brim of his hat politely.

He got into his cruiser, which was still running, and I stuffed the papers into my coat pocket ..

"Is this the right one?" Emmy had waited next to me and then held them up.

"Yes, honey."

"What did the police man want?"

"He was just asking if I lived here" I was thinking, *"I'd like to continue to..."*

"He didn't seem very happy— for it being almost Christmas." She observed.

"Well, he has a hard job to do, doesn't he?"

We finished putting up the lights and I brought out a huge wreath I'd made the year before and attached it to a heavy nail that handily protruded from just the right spot on the pink clapboard siding beneath the brass lantern porch light. It had lovely large pink poinsettias on it with a huge wine-colored bow. It was grand. So we went out and stood by the arbor, which I also put white lights on, and admired our teamwork. It was just stunning.

After we went inside, she made a cup of tea and we sat reading on the loveseat, me with my book and her with her fairy tales.

Not only was I at a loss as to who I could talk to about my situation, but I was also facing a crisis of faith with my children. They were questioning God and me.

One afternoon, I was in the study scraping candle wax from the brick hearth where I usually grouped a dozen pillar candles, and I could hear them talking in the dining room. So often on a Saturday night, people would gather around the fireplace, filled as it was with candles, and it really felt like a real fire. As I came through the foyer and toward the dining room with a coffee mug, one of them asked me,

"Why is it we're having such a hard time, Mom? What about all those times when you put *your* tithe in the collection plate? I thought that if you were doing something for God that He would bless you—or at least take care of you?"

Honestly, all I could do is tell them to have faith. One of them mumbled something about "seeing is believing" as I walked through the foyer back into the living room. . I told them I didn't have an answer for them, but that I was quite certain faith was believing without seeing.. I was praying so loud in my head that I thought they surely must be able to hear me, but I was desperate for them to hold on to the faith they had. It was three days before Christmas. There were no presents, and just enough in groceries for the next few days. Guests would be arriving in three hours and I had to finish the preparations be for I went to the grocery. I had seven dollars and thirty eight cents to buy what I would serve an unknown number of guests that night.

I vacuumed the carpets in the study and living room, and went into the foyer to put the vacuum away when I saw something red lying on the rug in front of the door. I walked over and picked it up thinking it was part of Emmy's craft-of-the-moment.

It was an envelope. There wasn't an address, just my name. I hadn't even heard the mail slot open. Puzzled, I opened it up. There was a Christmas card inside—and a check for a fifteen hundred dollars! I couldn't believe what I was seeing!

"Girls, you might want to come and take a look at this." There was the usual shuffling and teen-age wise cracks, but when they reached the French doors from the foyer into the living room, they looked at my face and then at the piece of paper with bewilderment. I held it forward and they looked down at the small writing. Suddenly wide-eyed wonder replaced their tired expression.

"Who *is* it, mom?"

"I don't know, Emmy. I don't recognize the name."

"Okay, I take back what I said—about the collection plate thing."

An hour and twenty minutes later I came up the basement stairs into the hallway carrying a navy and green plaid Christmas tablecloth for the dining room table Something caught my eye on the floor. There was another envelope on the rug and in it another card—this time with five hundred dollars! I called the girls down stairs and they looked more incredulous than before.

"What's going on anyway?"

"I think it's weird."

"I don't have a clue, girls. I didn't think anyone even knew about my job."

There was yet another envelope after dark, with two hundred and fifty dollars and a cheery little hand-made card.

I later came to believe that Gary and Marianne, the neighbors across the street, had a distinct hand in it. I am sure of it. They were the rare kind of neighbors that make a community worth living in and fighting for. It isn't the over-development of farmer's land that makes great places to live. It is all too often the trend of city councils, planning departments and greedy developers to overbuild in an area with the blind idea that *any* growth is good growth—and then move on, leaving the small towns to deal with overcrowding of the schools and lack of adequate water treatment, etc. It is as if we worship Growth at the expense of quality.

It is the people who live in communities and raise their families there that make all the difference. It is in the kindness shown by those good people in times of hardship that gives meaning to the lives of those who make small towns and villages a community.

If you don't believe me, try it. Sometime when you have a little extra money (or *especially* if you feel sorry for yourself that you don't have *more* money) and there's a soldier, an elderly lady, or a young single mom in front of you in the checkout with just a few items, offer to pay for their purchase. See what they'll do. Tell them it's your good deed for the day so you can eat chocolate the rest of the week. Tell the man in uniform that since he's putting his life on the line it's the least you can do.

Just make something up.

At first they'll look at you incredulously. Then a slight smile will light up their face. Then, the cashier will think you're nuts, and after them, the bagger. Pretty soon, three or four people are being blessed by just one small action on your part, and that doesn't include the people they will tell, "Hey, guess what happened today? Someone in the checkout paid for my groceries" If you can do it at Christmas time, then you can do it at other times too. Just bring Christmas Spirit with you wherever you go.

To have *that* kind of fun, you have to be daring. You have to be a swashbuckler. You can't be worried about your image or appearing to be odd.

It *is,* after all, **Christianity**, you know.

I would have to say that that Christmas was the most meaningful and blessed Christmas I remember. But it was not for presents, or even the funds that it was blessed, but for the goodness demonstrated by dear neighbors and the *faith* rekindled by those brightly colored envelopes.

Chapter 10

Cotton is his name. I don't remember what he said his given name was, and it doesn't really matter because he's been Cotton all his life. I found him to be the most annoying, loud, abrasive and outrageous person I'd ever met.

You never really knew what he would say, especially in mixed company.   He has proposed to about forty women in the three years that I knew him, and that was just on Saturday night. He was mid sixty-ish and still handsome, though the years and the mileage had taken their toll. He usually walked in at about eight-thirty, and smelled of aftershave— *Brut,* I think. He was tall and wore wire-framed glasses with his hair combed back. He wore blue jeans and usually sneakers, though I might have seen him in boots once or twice.

A wildcat from the hills of Kentucky, Cotton was a hell-raiser from way back. His family migrated here during the Second Great War because they were conscientious objectors and had been so ridiculed in their hometown that it was necessary to flee. People threw eggs and spit in those days. So to Ohio they came, and settled in South Lebanon. I think his dad was a preacher. Of all the brothers and sisters, Cotton was the black sheep, at least that is how a lot of his family referred to him. He is also the only one to serve in the armed forces. They all were deeply religious and took it quite seriously. Perhaps it had more to do with being embarrassed by him. A few of them liked to remind Cotton of that fact too, while pointing out the error of his ways, he told us— with the exception of his mother, who always saw the good in Cotton. It was her view that some folk make their way to the Lord through a long process, but are truer servants in the end because they know what they have been saved *from*.

He had been a teamster and a union steward. He drank and chased women. And he had been in politics—"'bout the only Democrat in Warren County", he'll tell you. "I've lost every time I've run, but that's because I didn't play dirty. I'd win the next time, because I know all the tricks now."

He slept every day until noon, and afterwards would go to Frisch's Big Boy Restaurant, where he would sit at one of the counter stools and eat lunch with the old guys. After three or four cups of coffee, and having made at least half a dozen church people indignant, he would head on over to Wal-Mart leaving a path of mayhem behind him everywhere.

He had never been in one of Wal-Mart's Snack Bars before, so one day he thought he'd give it a try. In a half-hour, he said he saw people he hadn't seen in *years* walk by. Since he had such a loud voice, he was usually able to get their attention. They would be initially startled, but then recognize him.

"Cotton? Is that *you*?" they would ask, then they would shake hands and sit a while and talk.

It then became part of Cotton's daily routine to make his way over to Wal-Mart after alienating half the folks at Frisch's.

In between long-lost acquaintances, he would get the regular denizens of the Wal-Mart Snack Bar in an uproar over some outrageous comment or question.

" Why do you think women usually outlive men?"

After four or five responses and conjectures, one older woman, who usually sat in silence, spoke up. "I'll tell you why women live longer—it's because those old fools are too darn sorry to exercise!"

Now, stop and consider this. When was the last time you were in a public place—like a restaurant— *and everyone in the restaurant was involved in the same conversation?* Doesn't everyone usually sit with someone— or by themselves— and they are enveloped in their isolation. Sitting in a room *full* of people, and yet the others in the room might just as well be additional plants or chairs for all that matter.

The whole scene was repeated time after time, and pretty soon, people started going to the snack bar just so they could join in whatever shenanigans Cotton had stirred up. They were forgotten people. Lonely people. Men and women whose days had drifted into a dreary monotony of making ends meet on a retirement pension, and waiting for their children to call, waiting for their children to come home. Some were in wheelchairs. Most were handicapped by a certain mindset of fate.

They had forgotten they had an opinion, mostly because no one ever asked them theirs. Yet Cotton was single-handedly able to bring all of these forgotten souls, these fellow black sheep— back to life. It was like he was raising the dead.

And it happened *every day*.

He told me that a few months after he started visiting the snack bar, that the manager had approached him.

"I've noticed that you come in here a lot," he said.

"Yeah?" Maybe Cotton was preparing himself for what the manager would say—probably nothing he wanted to hear...

"Well, Mr.- uh, Mr...."

"Cotton – ' name's Cotton.

"Mr. Cotton, I—"

"No! Not *Mister* Cotton— just Cotton. That's my first name. Cotton Amburgy."

"Oh." Replied the manager. "You related to Cash Amburgy?"

Cotton smiled. At one time he had been fed up with being Cash's brother—as if his only value or identity was being the brother of a famous radio preacher/appliance salesman. But that was a lifetime ago, when he was a younger and, I would add, a less-wise man. He understood that the young man meant no harm—Cotton had outgrown his indignation like the shirts of his younger years. Still smiling down at the manager, he nodded.

"He's my brother."

"I remember his commercials. Well, I was thinking. You know, we've never actually *had* a greeter for the Snack Bar before. I've seen how you just kind of warm up to everyone."

"Yeah?"

"How would you like to be our official Snack Bar Greeter? Of course, we'd give you a badge with your name— and title on it."

"That'd be okay." Cotton said. "Only one thing…" He pushed his glasses up on his nose, adjusting them.

"What would that be?"

"I don't really want to wear a badge."

"Mr. Amburgy," the manager smiled. "That would be just fine."

They shook hands and that was how Cotton became the only Snack Bar Greeter for Wal-Mart.

Cotton's most intriguing quality was his youthfulness of mind, for he never lost the natural curiosity of children that propels them onward to explore the world. Countless times Cotton would initiate a conversation on a Saturday night with, "I learned something new this week" or, "I tried doing something this week I've never done before." It often struck me how many folks will go on and on for years without ever learning anything new.

Cotton was never happier than when he was in the middle of a self-inflicted tempest, and it was never more evident than on a Saturday night at The Open Door Café.

That would have been enough to say about him. But there is something else about Cotton that people should know and it just might embarrass him to read it here. There were many times when groups of seven or eight people or as many as twenty— people of considerable means— came into my home during the years of The Open Door Café. They drank the coffee and ate the desserts and hors d'ouevres, but didn't contribute anything to the coffee house kitty in the front hallway—even though they were more than able and knew that I operated the cafe, being a single mom, at a loss.

They also became regularly indignant at Cotton.

When Cotton was there on a Saturday night, which was *every* Saturday night, except the one weekend a year when his family had a reunion, there was *always* a ten-dollar-bill in the cut-glass donation bowl.

In telling you this, I'm going to address a topic here that ought to be preached in churches. It's going to offend some people, maybe it will offend you—but it needs to be addressed. There are some Super Christians out there who ought not let anyone know they are a Christian at all. They are actually doing more harm to the faith than they realize. They should take the fish off the back of their car, and tuck their cross necklace inside until they learn to be a more courteous driver and act in a more loving way. They are doing more harm to the kingdom of God than a hundred "heathens".

I know I'm stepping on some toes here, and if you're cringing or feeling offended, you may be detecting that this truth applies to you. You need to consider what impression you are leaving with those you are trying to "convert". I know what I'm writing is true, because I've listened to servers (some of them *are* Christians) and I have *been* the server. In the majority of restaurants, NO ONE wants to work on a Sunday. Why? Because "The Church People" come in after services are over, and they are notoriously inconsiderate and high maintenance, demanding and sending items back (in the "nicest way", of course, but always with that slight edge to their voice of dissatisfaction and haughtiness) ——and then being stingy with the tip. They pride themselves on being at church every Sunday and crossing items off the Good Christian Checklist, and yet are blatantly unloving and selfish.

What *would* Jesus do? He'd probably put on an apron and help the server wait on you! Better yet, if He was sitting at the table, He would reach deep in His pocket and leave a tip that would *floor* the server! He would *not*, however, leave a tract on the table that looks like a $20— and nothing else.

Yes, we as Christians know that nothing is as precious as eternal life, and the salvation message is worth far more than any gold. But some Christians despise the cross by using it as an excuse to be cheap.

Walk in generosity. It *behooves* you as a Christian.

Over the years, Cotton has gotten a little slower, a little grayer and has lost brothers and sisters. I still see him occasionally, mostly when I'm at Wal-Mart, and it has occurred to me that he is one of the most interesting, loveable, young-hearted and precious men I have ever been privileged to know. And of all the *Christians* I know, I would have to say that Cotton often acts the most like one. He is real, he is hopelessly flawed and he knows it.

I venture to guess that some of you religious folk reading this know Cotton— or someone like him, and that perhaps you might have some uncomplimentary opinions of him. Maybe you know some things he did in his younger years that he might regret. But I guarantee that there is a Cotton in every one of us.

I most assuredly *hope so.*

Chapter 11

There's just something about a dead animal that brings out the best in a man.

All those tales of knights slaying dragons can't compare to dragin' dead animals out of crawl spaces and such. Guys *love* it.

It was a Saturday evening late in May, a perfect spring day, warm and sunny. I had just finished cutting the grass and was trimming around the stairs to the deck so guests could sit outside if they liked. In an hour and a half people would start arriving for the café. The quiche was out of the oven, all golden brown along flaky crust, there were fresh strawberries in crepes in the fridge. Even the coffee was brewed. All I would need to do before people began to arrive was finish the trimming and take a shower.

I was just finishing the spot by the planter of geraniums when I noticed what I (at first) thought was a dog, lying in the grass by the lattice that surrounded the deck. My first reaction was that maybe it had been hit by a car on our busy street (known as The Highway to Heaven—cats feared it and dogs crossed it hurriedly in reverence), but when I looked closer, I saw the rat-like tail of everyone's favorite woodland creature, the opossum. It was the biggest one I'd ever seen! *And* it was bloated.

It was all becoming clear to me now— the plethora of iridescent green flies I'd seen all over the deck and the pungent smell of rotting flesh— it had to be a dead thing.

What could I do? It was wedged in there pretty good. *"I can't let people come out here!"* I thought. There wasn't time for me to deal with the carcass *and* get ready.

I peeled off my tan gardening gloves and tossed them on the top step as I ascended the stairs. *"I'll just have to deal with it tomorrow after church. That's the only thing I can do."* I thought. *"Only it'll be another day older..."*

I went inside and took a shower, finger-combed my hair and put some makeup on. I would be ready in plenty of time.   S o — why is it that I could *still* smell the old 'possum Down Under?

"Must be my imagination." I rationalized. I went downstairs and put on some music. *"Yes, um...let's see— Dave Brubeck and maybe Nightnoise. Woah! Is the smell really that strong?*

I lit candles—lots of 'em. And incense, too— in every room. The whole place was *ablaze.*

Suddenly the doorbell rang.

"Now who could that be—" I said out loud. "Smoky the Stupid *Bear*?!"

I looked outside through the lace curtain, hoping that it would be the little neighbor boy wanting to clean out the garage, mow the lawn, or better yet, remove a dead animal. I knew by the fact that they rang the bell that they were first time visitors to the café— everyone else knew that at the Open Door Café, you just walked in. But it was four ladies who had come in a van from...what did the license say? Indi*ana*!?

"Oh *no*! They couldn't possibly have come this early! The coffeehouse doesn't even start for another thirty-five minutes. Don't they have *homes* to go to?" I muttered out loud.

I couldn't suggest they take a look around downtown or something because they weren't from the area. There was nothing else to be done but fling the door open.

"Why the heck do you think I call it the Open Door Café?" I said laughing. "Come on in ladies!"

They looked startled at first, but it broke any ice there could have been and they themselves started laughing.

"Is this the singles' function?" one of them inquired, stepping into the foyer. "We were expecting a shop, weren't we girls? This is a... well, a *home*. We wanted to come early to check it out."

I was glad they were all wearing ample amounts of cologne.

"Actually, girls, you don't *really* have to ring the bell for the café, you just walk right in on in. What's your name?"

"We wanted to come early. Oh—I'm Lenore and this is Anita, and Willa, and Edith.

"Well, I'm so glad you could visit." I shook all their hands-except Lenore, who only would go as far as shaking finger-*tips.*

I have a theory about finger-tip shakers. I have a feeling that you can never really count on them— just as they pull their hand back at the last instant before you can take their full hand in yours, it seems that they will always back out on you at the last minute. It always gives me the willies to get a fingertip shaker.

"Here, you can put your purses down by the foot of the steps and we can sit in here" I gestured toward the living room—which, incidentally, was the room *farthest* away from the back deck. If I closed both the pocket doors and the French doors, well, that would make the living room pretty much impenetrable to the intrusion of any outside odors... Kind of like a bunker.

"Are you sure they'll be alright?" Edith whined, looking warily about, as if House Creepers would snatch her millions.

"Well, for eight months people have been leaving their purses here— and there's only the five of us…and we can see the hall from in here."

They laughed nervously but sat their purses down, except Edith.

"If you'll excuse me, I was just going to fill the cream pitcher up. I'll be right back. Just take a seat, ladies." I always liked to leave guests alone for a moment to compose themselves and

I went into the kitchen, going through the motions of filling the cream pitchers but my mind was consumed by The Uninvited critter was still outside. Why, I felt as if I could *still* smell him— even though I was inside. I took two white china cream pitchers off the shelf and filled them both with half-and-half then carried them into the study. I glanced into the living room where the ladies were lined up primly on the couch like little 'possums—er, birds, on a wire.

"You have a lovely home—did you decorate it yourself?" Edith was still clutching her purse in a death grip.

"Well, actually I grew up with all this stuff. This is my grandmother in this oval picture…"

"Oh dear, what is that *smell*?" Exclaimed Anita.

I panicked. "Oh, dear! What does it smell like?"

"Like something *burning*— is it incense?"

"Well, yes…don't you love it? " I was so relieved I felt giddy.

"I'm *deathly* allergic to incense… can you put it out?"

"Oh, of course." I went about extinguishing all the incense. *"Now, how can anyone wear that much perfume and yet be allergic to incense?"* I wondered. I was in a bad mood now but it really didn't have anything to do with the ladies on the couch, rather, it was the grisly guest hanging out under my deck.

"Would you like some coffee? I have everything right in here"

"I don't like coffee." Willa sniffed. "We never really *drink* coffee, do we girls?"

"Oh, no." They called from the other room in varying degrees of unison. They sat there silently. All I could hear was the drum solo from *Take Five* and the ticking of the grandfather clock.

"This is going to be a long evening." I thought. Then, "Oh, you know, I completely forgot— I have tea."

"I don't drink tea either. Don't you have anything *without* caffeine?"

"I have *just* the thing—herbal tea! There are several kinds to choose from." I led them *en mass*, like the Pied Piper, into the study where I had the refreshments.

"Why, isn't that clever! Look Anita—she put her coffeepot in that armoire! I've never seen anything like *that*." They all started chattering away, trying to decide is they wanted Cranberry Cove or Mandarin Orange Spice or any one of five other flavors.

"Look, Lenore, there's little sugar cubes!"

"It's just like a tea party!" I offered.

I heard the front door open without anyone ringing the bell. *"That would be one of the regulars."* I thought and excused myself.

Coming into the foyer I could see it was Cotton.

"He-e-y, Cotton— how the heck are you?"

"Fine, Caron—you?"

"Just busy—the usual. Hey, I could use your help. There are some ladies in here from out of town and I need you to break the ice a little. I think they need a big dose of Cotton Amburgy… can you…?"

"I'll handle it" he laughed, hiking up his belt. I could always count on Cotton to liven things up, though there was no telling what he would say. We went in to where the girls were stirring honey into their tea and I introduced them to Cotton. Immediately, he said something so outrageous that they all lost it and nearly spilled their collective Constant Comment Decaf.

The front door opened and I peeked around the corner into the hallway—what a relief! It was Steve. At an opportune moment I could ask him what to do about the critter. He always had good advice on guy stuff.

"Hey, Caron, how are you?"

"Hi, Steve. Come on in." Then I slipped into the foyer glancing behind me. He frowned and looked at me inquisitively.

"I have a problem…" and in hushed tones I told him about the 'possum.

"YOU'VE GOT A DEAD *WHAT*?" It was Cotton.

Now, why couldn't he hear you when you were talking right *at* him, but could hear just fine now— and he had to say it at the top of his lungs?

"Oh, hi, Steve—how's it goin'?"

"He—e-y-y, Brother Cotton—" Steve and Cotton shook hands.

"Dead '*POS*SUM? Willa, there's a dead 'POSS-um!"

Lenore acted as if she thought it would rise from the dead, open the door and leap onto her neck in a fit of rabid angst.

"Did you hear that? She's got a dead 'possum!" Edith howled.

Great. Now the possum was out of the body bag.

"Hold it, everyone! Just calm down." I tried to speak in a soothing manner though I was really annoyed. " It's outside under the deck"

"Okay, Caron." Steve said in loud false bravado tones. "I guess I can get it out of there. Has it been there long?"

"Kinda— I think." I grimaced. "Really— you needn't—I can do it myself. Just tell me what to *do* with it."

"Is it… is it *smelly*?" Steve was wincing. The old boy was committed now and he knew it.

"Well…"

He straightened his 6"3' frame and gathered up all the Italian nerve he could muster.

"Show me where it is." he said— dead serious. I nearly laughed out loud. He looked like a gunslinger from an old western. I felt guilty having him deal with my dead animal. Why couldn't he just let dead 'possums lie?

"Yeah, *Steve*'ll take care of it, Caron." Cotton volunteered. What a trooper. "Hey girls, did I tell you I used to be in politics?" Cotton was on a roll— the only trucker-turned-politician in a flock of spinsters. The streets of Lebanon, Ohio were safe now. I slipped my shoes on and got a flashlight out of the junk drawer. I don't know what I was going to do with it, but it gave me an added air of confidence.

I led the way out the back door onto the deck and down the stairs. I turned as he reached the bottom step.

"Steve—he's not of this earth."

"Whew!" His eyes crossed and he shook his head.

"I told you it was bad."

He went around to the side and with a quick jerk, pulled off the lattice panel that screened the underside of the deck. I didn't even know the lattice *came* off— but it was off now.

"It looks like he tried to get under the deck and got stuck there beside the corrugated drain... is that from the downspout?'

"Yeah. What a way to go." I mused.

I pushed on the drain with my foot— and it seemed to dislodge the carcass! It slid forward, and was now far enough under the deck to get a grip on it—if that was what one wanted to do. Steve went into the garage and got a snow shovel.

"Have you got a black trash bag?"

Without a word, I ran inside and got the whole roll. I figured we could do layers.

When I reached the bottom of the steps, he was looking a little green (Steve— not the 'possum).

"I know— it's pretty bad."

He tried to get close enough to the deck to slide the snow shovel underneath "It", but the smell drove him back.

We almost gagged standing there, the idea of a living 'possum was bad enough, but just thinking of the greasy fur, the tail... those little pink feet with the claws.... He walked away, and I followed him.

"Caron, go inside, I'll handle It." he said bravely.

I knew it was all an act. Nobody wants to do what I was asking him to do.

"I can't let you do this. It's too much to ask." I leaned up against the garage. The smell was less oppressive there.

"I can get the shovel under him—if he comes up all in one piece, we're good," The thought of 'possum parts remaining on the ground while part of him was in the shovel was just revolting.

I nodded. 'Hey, you know what? He's like Lazarus, Steve!" I started laughing, I called out in brave deep tones, "'Possum come *FORTH*!"

The thought of the little guy creeping out from under the deck in shrouds was too much. Especially with the aroma.

We laughed in loud guffaws and doubled over. "Hey, Steve, what perfume do you think that is—'Lilly of the ***ALLEY?***'"

We just lost it. We were like two ten-year-olds throwing rotten apples at bees.

Then amid the frivolity, I looked up at him and grimaced. "I feel awful that you're doing this. This is the kind of thing you can only ask of a total stranger—someone who gets *paid* to do this stuff."

"Caron, I can't let you deal with this by yourself. Come on. We'll hold our breath. You hold the bag open and I'll drop him in."

The sides kept drooping inward and I had visions of the 'possum hitting my arm as it descended into the inky blackness of the plastic bag.

"It's too big— he won't fit!" I wailed as I started feeling light-headed from lack of oxygen. I stood up. "Wait! I know! We'll put the bag in a *box*. There's one in the garage."

Steve flung open the garage door, and it sent Sadie Bunny (who had gotten out of her cage) scurrying for cover. We got the box and opened it up wide, filling it with the opened trash bag.

Steve lifted the 'possum again with the snow shovel and it was poised on the very edge. There were tears in the corners of our eyes and he couldn't hold the weight of the 'possum up on the drooping end of the shovel any longer. It slid off the end and hit the ground onto its stiff little feet, and then, hovering vertically for a glorious three seconds, it flopped over on its side, rocked slightly, and lay still. It almost looked as if it really *would* rise from the dead!

We *howled!* Every time we pulled ourselves together, one of us would start laughing again and that would set the other one off. Our sides were aching and we were coughing. Then, suddenly I looked up at the window and saw that the kitchen was *full* of *people* looking out the back window! Spectators jostled for a look and looked between the shoulders and heads of the others. All the regulars were there, pointing and laughing.

Steve saw my face and turned to see them there, crowded together so they could watch the spectacle. We could hear them laughing from outside.

More determined than ever, and with a deft push, he managed to slide the shovel once more under the possum and scooping him up handily, dropped him into the bag. Then, with lightening speed, he folded the flaps shut on the box and straightened upright and held his arms up in a triumphant touchdown signal. You'd think he roped a critter at the 'Possum Rodeo".

There were cheers and applause from the kitchen and they rushed out the back door, only to be confronted by the lingering aroma.

They stopped dead in their tracks.

"Wow, that's bad!"

"I'm goin' back inside!"

"Hey, Steve, I've got a dead snake in my cistern." Someone suggested. "Maybe you could—"

"Not a *chance*." Steve warned.

He took the Box 'o Possum out to his truck to dispose of in the Dumpster at his apartment building. I went inside and sat down at the dining room table. I needed to compose myself. My knees were shaking and all I wanted was to get inside away from the smell.

In a moment Steve came in and sat down at the table. The setting sun of that early May shone in the window and against the wall behind him. I was staring at the table.

"Caron. Look, I *know* how hard it is to do what you're doing. My mom raised five of us boys by herself. You can't pretend it isn't tough. You don't really have to do everything by yourself, you know."

"Steve, there just isn't anyone to help—most of the time. There have even been times when I *have* asked and people were too busy—or just didn't want to be bothered. I just don't want to be disappointed —I don't want to impose. So I tend to do everything myself." My voice shook but I tried to stop it.

"I know. I'm the same way." he reached out and patted my hand. "Hey now, quit— you're going to make me cry too." He was smiling but there were tears in his eyes.

"You may have had that experience before, but it won't happen every time. If you ever need help again, would you just let me know?"

I nodded, looking down at my hands, still a little shaky from the 'possum rodeo.

There were times after that that I asked his help and he was true to his word. That night I learned that it was okay to ask for help, that it was okay to admit a need.

And it wasn't Cotton Amburgy, but the *'possum* who broke the ice.

Chapter 12

Molly Healy.

She was there from the very beginning. She was petite with small hands and small features. Even her feet were small and she would slip her shoes off and push them under a chair or into a corner to go in her stockinged feet. She was, in reality really shy, but made an effort to make sure everyone was having a good time, though usually she helped in the kitchen with final preparations.

That's what all the shy people did. They would make a *beeline* for the kitchen to ask if I needed any help. It was so much easier than sitting down in one of the chairs and entering into a full-blown conversation with a total—or almost total—stranger. Making themselves busy was the surest diversion from the torture of introducing oneself and striking up a conversation. I usually tried to discourage people from doing just that—at least long term. Once they had something to bring to the buffet in the living room or to the dining room table they were fine. It was just getting there that posed the problem.

Molly was generally quiet and preferred the background to the limelight. It was generally late in the evening, after some of the guests had actually left for the evening, that she might slip into a chair at the large dining room table with a cup and saucer. She would tuck her feet under her and settle in to listen.

It was not that she was closed off from people, for you could see in her dark brown eyes the open heart of someone who had a deep empathy for their struggles. She was genuinely moved by the things shared in confidence and unconditional acceptance among friends there in the soft glow of the chandelier. At times she offered encouraging suggestions or an affirmation, which she did fearlessly, though at times her voice caught in her throat. Watching her, you could tell that it was hard for her to overcome her natural reserve, but as she would look intently into their faces, you knew that she knew their very heart, and the whole room would silence, because it was rather seldom that she said anything at all.

Have you ever noticed that a lot of people act as if complimenting or encouraging someone else or building up another's self-esteem *costs* them something, or somehow depletes their own reserve of self-esteem? As Christians, it seems to me we ought to be the most lavish with our praise and affirmations of others. It's not as if we have a limited supply or anything. If Christ calls our hearts His dwelling place, and He embodies all of creation and eternity, then surely we can dish out a few compliments now and then, right?

Molly seemed able to draw from a deep well within herself a drink of cold water for the parched soul, a word of understanding, the frequent hug, and at times she simply rested her hand on theirs.

It was as though some place within her *shared* that place of mourning or wonder or confusion She just seemed to be the kind of person that everyone tended to share their sorrow or their questions at life's mysteries with; and there was always a look of relief in their eyes that someone at that table understood and really *knew* them.

They were *known*. Someone took the time and made the effort to know them— quite possibly one of humankind's greatest needs; and there was a resonance in her with their wounded spirit.

Month after month she remained the quiet and unobtrusive comrade of the friends of the cafe, and yet during that time, she herself had remained a mystery.

Until one night in early June.

There was only a small group that night since there were several relatives of the usual patrons either graduating, getting married, or going on vacation. It had been mildly warm until the sun went down. Although some us had been sitting outside on the deck, everyone came inside as the late spring chill settled between the houses.

Cotton had refilled his mug and pulled out a chair at the dining room table.

"Hey, it looks like a small crowd tonight. Maybe we can all fit around this table," commented Phil. "I'll get a couple of chairs from the kitchen. We can fit." He was the perennial optimist.

Molly had gone into the living room and returned a moment later with two trays from the buffet, one of cookies, and another with little fruited cheesecakes. She placed them on the table and got her own cup, which she had left on the kitchen counter. She waited in the doorway of the kitchen, leaning against the white painted door jamb.

"*Now* you're talkin,'" Gary quipped. He was quite the cook himself, and often brought treats to share.

It was good to be inside where it was warm, I thought, and also where it was easier to hear. Out on the deck there was too much competition from the traffic and the singing of spring tree frogs. Eventually, everyone found a seat around the heavy sugar maple table that, incidentally, had seen many a pie crust rolled out and the ghosts of Christmas Cookies Past.

"Does it *really* seem like we've been meeting like this for over a year and a half now? It seems to me like we've all known each other a lot longer." Steve observed, then laughing, added, "I guess you could take that more than one way."

Everyone laughed. Turning to face Molly, he continued, "You know, for months we've been sharing who we are and what's going on in *our* lives, but we don't really know anything about *you*. Come over here and sit with us." The only seat left was on my grandpa's old green tool chest, so Steve pulled it away from the wall.

"He's right," added Phil. "You've been listening to all of us go on and on about ourselves for months—*some* of us more than others." He nodded toward Cotton in jest, to which Cotton grinned back, acknowledging the humor. He was always such a good sport.

There was no escape. Not with seven pairs of eyes meeting hers. Not with expectancy hanging in the air above the chandelier and reaching into the corners of the room.

She reddened and looked down at her coffee cup, and gulped. "Yikes! I don't really know where to begin," she said quietly. "I don't have anything 'prepared'." She said her heart was beating so loud in her ears and throat, she felt like she couldn't hear. She came close and took a seat on the old green toolbox, then looked up and met the gazes from the friends she had grown to know over the past months. They were waiting.

Finally, Molly summoned her nerve, drawing a deep breath, then laughed a little, flustered. "Where do you want me to begin?"

"Well, the beginning's always good. Where are you from?" Cotton was good at breaking the awkward silences that seem to precede the first tenuous steps into someone's inner world.

"Okay... I'm originally from Columbus, but I came to Cincinnati when I was twelve, after my dad was nearly killed in an industrial accident. He then went to work for the University of Cincinnati."

"Did he teach there?"

"Mm hmm. He taught in the Chemical and Nuclear Engineering Department. He was a really interesting man—I think I learned a lot from him. He had not graduated from college himself, but was self-taught—and he was good at teaching others..."

"He never graduated from college? And he taught Chemical and Nuclear *Engineering*?"

"Or high school. We talked his parents into allowing him to go into the service. It was at the end of World war II."

"What is the most important thing you learned from your dad?" Rick pressed.

"I feel like I'm being interviewed or something." She thought a moment. "To try new things. To teach yourself how to do things. If you're determined enough, you can teach yourself most anything. And mostly how to persevere. He had overcome some obstacles in his life. He struggled for a long time with alcohol. He wasn't always likeable, but toward the end of his life, he seemed to pull it together. Shortly before he died he made a real effort to know me as an adult. By then I already had four children of my own."

"Isn't it weird how your parents don't ever seem like they would be your friends when you're young, but then— after they grow up a little..." Gary interjected, smiling.

"Yeah, they seem a whole lot more agreeable." Cotton added and we all laughed because most of us were working our way through the adolescence of our own children.

"Well, like I said, we got along fine right before he died. The last time I saw him, he told me he wanted to have lunch— that there was something he wanted to talk to me about. He told me to call him on

Wednesday and we would plan a time. That was on a Thursday and he died five days later."

"You don't know what he wanted to tell you?" asked Steve.

"No. I wanted to tell him something, though. He didn't know I was expecting my fifth and youngest child. She is the only one of my children who never saw her grandfather. The kids always called him Grandpa Whiskers because he had a white beard. He looked like a sea captain.

"I did, however tell him the *most* important thing before he died."

"What's that?" Cotton was leaning forward.

She smiled and replied, "'I love you.' I think it's really important to tell people regularly that you love them. You may never get another chance."

"And what about your mom? Is she still living?" inquired Phil.

"No. She's passed on too."

"Oh. So both of your parents are gone... and your marriage?"

She straightened a little, grimacing.

"Uh, you don't have to tell us if you don't want to." Steve offered quickly. "Let's talk about something else." He straightened in his chair, taking a sip out of his coffee mug while feigning disinterest. We all laughed, as he exaggerated the act of drinking he coffee, holding his pinky finger high.

"No. It's all right. You guys have all been so open with me and entrusted me with all *your* stories and fears. I'm just not sure you want to hear—." She sighed with resignation. "Okay. I'll tell you because there's such a small group here— and only because I want you to know what God has done in my life. You have to promise you won't feel— well, I don't want anyone feeling sorry for me. What I mean is that it isn't a pretty tale. The only reason I'm telling you is because you asked."

You could hear a Kleenex drop.

She proceeded to relate how she had gotten married with all the hopes that it would be a Christian marriage. She had wanted so much to be the wife he would be proud of; that when he was talking with his coworkers that he would praise her for being creative or industrious— not 'the old ball and chain". All she had ever wanted was a normal life; normal in the sense of being free of the fear she had grown up with in the shadow of her father's alcoholic rages. She did not want a Super-Christian, but simply a Christian man who cared about God and his own personal growth of character. If those two things were preeminent in his mind, then she knew that they could conquer any problem that arose in life.

However, her fifteen-year marriage turned out to be much different than her young woman's dreams. It seemed that the harder she tried to be a good wife and mother, the more she taught herself, the harder she strove for his approval— or at least the absence of his *disapproval* and the resulting rage, the more angry he seemed to become. She knew she could not change him, so she tried to change herself. But for all the long years of her marriage, she lived with intimidation, physical abuse, wide, unpredictable mood swings, jealousy, control and rage. It was as if the entire time was spent in a 'flight or fight' syndrome, backed into a corner emotionally and sometimes physically. She would immediately tense when she heard his car in the driveway, and the rest of the evening would be spent in trying to avert an argument.

She was afraid to stay, but even more afraid to leave.

There were times, of course, when everything *seemed* great— like after an argument. It was like another honeymoon—at least it seemed that way compared to the oppressive atmosphere leading up to an argument. It was like a roller coaster of extreme highs and terrifying lows. When he was in a good mood she felt so relieved that she would do almost anything to extend the tenuous peace. Often the abuse took the form of drawing her into an argument. The baiting and bullying would build like a thunderstorm— with each comment more intimidating or degrading that the one before it—until she said something back in defense of herself. Her retort would then unleash tirades that lasted hours and usually included some form of physical abuse. She could have no difference of opinion, even in such trivial matters as movies or books.

She thought that even if she *did* leave, that the problem would never really go away, that she would only be the object of more rage. She had read of estranged husbands who stalked their former spouse and indeed that is what ultimately occurred; of worse things beyond that. But worse, there was the fear that her children would be stuck in the same situation she had left. She could escape, but they could not, because they would have weekly visitations. She feared that they would have to endure the same endless questioning and intimidation as a captive audience because they were too young to stand up for themselves. If she could not stop his behavior, how could she expect *them* to? If she was frightened by him, she knew that they were as well.

She had prayed for God to change her spouse, prayed in all the ways she had been advised in the Christian books and by well-meaning friends, all along hiding from her friends and family members the truth of what was really going on. But in the inevitable isolation that accompanies an abuse situation, there was no one to whom he was accountable, no one who could insist that the abuse stop. After all, the abuse never took place in front of anyone who could do anything about it. When she tried to tell family members or her pastor what was happening, he accused her of being disloyal and berated her for what he felt to be betrayal. He painted her disloyalty as more heinous than his bullying and abuse. He was the absolute and final authority in a closed kingdom shut off from the world and its mores. So she became good at pretending and defending.

She had sought help in the form of counseling, but was given the message that she should be more submissive, or that the abuse was somehow her fault— that there was an emotional payoff, or that she had to be patient. On one occasion, the counselor told her that the problem didn't develop overnight, and it wouldn't be solved overnight.

"I felt that I had no one in my corner, that I had given all I had left. Obviously, the counselors, a husband and wife team, had no clue what it was like to live in that environment. I had sought help to end the abuse, and yet I was being told I had to stay in it, where it was likely to happen again; or worse, that I somehow enjoyed it. I wondered how they could say that, when I'd come to them about solving the problem in the first place. The whole focus was on being understanding and compassionate toward her husband.

"There was nothing left in me to stay and wait until he resolved his issues. It seemed like a death sentence to me. I retreated into myself and became numb. I felt as if I existed and nothing more. It had been so hard to reach up and grasp a helping hand from what seemed a well of darkness and despair, and the helping hand seemed more concerned with cajoling the one who terrorized me."

None of the Christian sources she sought advised her to leave until he changed his behavior. There had not, at that time been the pioneering and widely publicized work on setting boundaries. She didn't have a clue as to what a boundary was.

"I tried to fight sinking deeper into despair, and one day, I remember standing in my bedroom at the dresser. I had put some clean laundry away, and as I closed the dresser drawer, I leaned against it and rested my head on my hands. I thought, *"I can't go on. I don't want to exist another day. What does my life hold, anyway? More of the same? I'll never be free of this, I will never be who I truly am. I will never have the chance to be what I was meant to be. I am losing every last bit of who I am, and every day I am giving up more ground, more of my Self. I can't take my life, because my children would be abandoned to a world of fear and tyranny.'* I couldn't abandon them, but I just didn't want to live any longer. I had to fight my way back from that place, standing at the gates of hell. I bit my lip and kept on going. The result is that I merely went through the motions of living.

"It was a few days later that I found out I was pregnant with my fifth child—only five months later, that fifth child, my daughter, was stillborn. It was just after Christmas, and a month after my nose was broken for the second time. I had to go to Brownie meetings with my lip split and my nose swollen. No one asked me what happened. I was invisible. How I wished someone had taken me aside and asked me if I needed help. But none of it was harder than the loss I was carrying instead of my baby.

"Of all the things in life, losing one of your children is the hardest. And it doesn't matter if you have other children. I would never hold *her*. There would be no first day of school, no prom dress. I wanted to name her, and have a Christmas ornament on the tree that was hers. There was nothing to hold, nothing to cuddle. There was only a flat stomach where only days before, had been my fifth child. And so, I folded up the maternity clothes and put them away.

"I was told by my husband after two days that I had to get over it. He told me I was turning into a basket case. 'I don't know, do you think you need psychiatric help?' he mocked, on the third day after it happened. It was so cruel, invasive and insensitive that I shut down entirely. I had no chance to cry or grieve— I had no way to work through losing my child. I didn't know anyone else that this had happened to. Eventually, I did go to a support group that became available for parents who lost children through stillbirth."

We were all silent, sitting there at that table. Some people stared at their hands or the candle in the center, others' eyes were riveted on her face, or her hands, with her fingers resting gently on the handle and the rim of her cup. We had asked for it, not knowing the depths it would take us all sitting there. We had asked for it, and we did not want what we had gotten.

We were *growing*, though, as a result. It *could* have been a cheerful conversation, properly superficial and empty of the pain of understanding the struggle of someone *else*. Life isn't always pretty, though, and yet once we realize that, beauty takes on a new meaning, as does kindness and compassion.

She continued quietly, looking at times at the candle and then at her cup. Occasionally she looked at the faces that met hers.

"Later that same year, the year I lost my baby— and the year my father died, I *did* have another baby, in November, a little girl, and I named her. She would have her own Christmas ornament on the tree, as did the infant girl I had lost. And I struggled through the following four more years."

I went back to work and in working found some of the self-esteem that had been eroded away."

One day, when she was at work, she saw a pamphlet lying on a counter, and while she waited for a pot of coffee to brew for the employee lounge area, she picked it up casually and started reading it. It was entitled, "The Cycle of Abuse". She looked about her. She had no idea where it had come from, except one of the other women in the office was in the process of a divorce. It would be a while before the other workers arrived, so she went into the ladies' room and read it as she leaned against the vanity. Tears welled up in her eyes as she realized she was reading about her own self. It was all there in the pamphlet, the honeymoon phase following an incident of abuse, the buildup of tension or the incident that sparked the argument, the form of abuse, the apology and promise of change and then the honeymoon again. She realized that for months when she thought of going home after work, she would feel sick with fear–she was filled with anxiety and her hands would be sweaty. While she was at work, she was safe and there were fellow adults she could interact with.

She thought of the fellow employees and how they talked of their wives with respect. She considered how she herself was treated by her coworkers and it seemed so .....*normal*. Working and being involved at her children's school gave her the opportunity step away from her situation at home and to see how bizarre and repressive her world had become, how isolated from friends and family they all were. The isolation provided the cover of darkness in which the abuse was able to continue.

That evening, she found herself trapped in yet another conversation in which she felt there would be no resolution. She would say whatever she could to placate him—anything to avoid another fight. The discussions always lasted for hours in a repetitious cycle. Her children came to the bedroom door to ask if she would make dinner. It was ten o'clock. Her husband flung open the door angrily to face her six year old and her four year old. She saw the faces of her children as they stood silently looking first at her and then at their father. The youngest was holding a small stuffed monkey and her blanket. The night before that, they had been upstairs for so long that her four year-old had fallen asleep with her blanket without eating dinner. Without a word they hung their heads and turned silently to go back downstairs. They knew she would not be making dinner again that night, and that they would have to make do with what they could get for themselves.

The next morning, she came in to work early and the room was empty. She sat down at her desk, with her face cupped in her hands and cried. She knew how desperate the whole picture was. She knew that she had to leave, if not for her own sake, then for the sake of the children she watched walk away from the bedroom door the night before.

She had born six children with a man she had not only never felt loved by, but whom she must fear. She knew it would be an incredibly hard life ahead of her as a single mother with five children; her oldest had just turned fifteen and her youngest had just turned four, but she had to have courage—not for herself, but for them. As hard as she knew it would be to support them all and build a new life that was safe, it was worth any price to be free. To remain any longer in the same situation was unconscionable— it would make her a party to their abuse to keep silent and stay.

"Why didn't you leave earlier, before things got so bad?" asked Cotton.

"Yeah, I would have left after the first time..." added Cathy.

"Everyone always asks me that. It isn't as easy as you would think. Even sitting here telling you this, I myself think, *"Why didn't I leave after the first incident?"* In the beginning, I thought it was fairly normal to argue. After all, I had grown up with it. I didn't have anything "normal" to compare my marriage to. I did love things about him. It's a very complex problem, and one you can't figure out necessarily on your own.

"Over the years, though, abuse seems to entrap you. You do love the person, after all, or you wouldn't be in the relationship. They aren't totally terrible— they do have good qualities, and that is where the dilemma comes in. You're under this pressure to be forgiving and understanding, especially if your Christianity is used by the abuser as leverage— to force you to forgive, or more accurately, *forget*. It's like this: If I were to wrap a thread around you, pinning your arms to your sides, you could easily break free. *But*, if I wrap it around you several hundred times, then it would become progressively harder to break free. Most people think that physical abuse is an isolated occurrence, but in fact it is incident after incident; *and,* it is a thousand smaller, seemingly insignificant instances of giving in, holding your tongue, and letting demeaning things slide by— just to keep the peace. The result is that your boundaries, your identity, is eroded away until you have nothing left to stand on. If you forgive everything, then you aren't allowed to bring it up again. If 'it's okay," then that becomes the standard. The abuser capitalizes on your acquiescence, and because you *do* let things slide, then it sends them the message that it's okay to do it again— or to do more— the next time. The challenge is then to increase the verbal abuse until they know they have hurt you. It becomes a cat and mouse game. And keeping you isolated insures that no one outside of the marriage will ever discover 'the game'."

Sitting there, we realized we were, at that moment getting a rare look inside a living nightmare, and able to see inside the world of abuse that enslaves so many—men as well as women and children. You read things like this in the paper or you see it on a movie of the week, but it is quite another thing to hear someone describe their own experience.

For all the years she had been in her marriage, she could never determine if she should admit she had made a mistake and leave, or realizing it, stay and persevere. She wanted to possess character, to not be a quitter; but was unsure whether behaving with character meant leaving or *staying*.

If anything was unclear up to that point, the looks on her children's faces told her everything she needed to know.

Cotton stood up and took her cup to refill it, and bringing it back, gently sat it on the table before her. She smiled up at him, and continued.

For a long time after the divorce she felt betrayed by God and she was angry with Him. Many times she thought of people down through the ages who were good people and yet struggled with the problem of evil. What of all the people in the concentration camps and missionaries who are martyred? She had wondered why, if she had followed "the rules", her life had turned out the way it had. Was it "her cross to bear?" Since she couldn't figure out the rules, she decided not to play. She didn't want anything to do with Him.

After a few years had passed, however, she longed for the sense of a state of grace. The longing for a state of grace, and somehow deep in her spirit, the knowledge that God actually *understood* her anger towards Him— and was big enough to handle it— is what wooed her back to Him.

For a while, she and her five children lived with her mother, since her father had passed away, but it was really difficult. So she found an inexpensive apartment owned by a coworker. For the entire time they lived in it, the bathroom sink was not attached to the drain pipe. It was a newly remodeled bathroom, but only half-completed. The kitchen sink didn't work very well either, as it had a gaping hole in the elbow pipe. She placed a bucket under the hole and emptied it when she needed to do the dishes. Eventually, the landlord fixed the kitchen sink pipe.

The main thing is, it was home and it was *peaceful*.

She knew she had to forgive everyone in her life who had ever hurt her, or she would never make any progress in her own growth, and would never be successful at anything.

More than anything, however, she knew that she needed to forgive God.

"What do you mean, you had to forgive *God*— I thought He's the one who does the forgiving. It seems arrogant to imply that God needs *our* forgiveness." asserted Phil.

"The person guarding the prisoners is very much a prisoner himself, wouldn't you agree?" she asked.

"Forgiveness is something different than just God forgiving our sins, or us forgiving someone else. It is not placing blame. It is not exacting retribution or payment of a debt that can never be repaid. Stop and think of it. You can never *un*-do what has been done. You can't *un*-say words that have been said. Only love, which defines the identity of God — lasts forever. It is the ultimate reality. Anything else may as well be an illusion. Love really does cover a multitude of sins.

"Forgiveness is living as if the offence never even happened. Forgiveness is like a lubricant that frees up the parts of a machine that have frozen. We get stuck in the past—our wounded hearts and tragic times—and it will affect other areas of our life until we get un-stuck.

"I had to realize that I might *never* have the answers I was looking for, I might *never* have an explanation for what went wrong. I had to become okay with that; I had to stop dwelling on the past and go on. I had to give up my 'right to know'. I never had thought of it before, but you have to forgive all kinds of *things* as well as people. You especially must forgive the *past*"

She was silent, as were we all. If it was uncomfortable for her to tell her story, it was even more so for us to listen. Who could have imagined that the diminutive woman who recounted in such a moving and compelling way the dark details of her marriage and the years of struggle afterward, was the one so moved by the trials of the other guests of the cafe. She always seemed unconcerned with her own problems. She seemed like the type who could overcome just about anything, but perhaps it was because *she had*.

After a while, Mark spoke. "Do you talk to your former spouse now?"

"Sometimes. At first, it was really hard because there was so much tension and animosity. I was trying very hard to set boundaries that had been so eroded that I lost who I was. We have agreed to disagree, but we're cordial to each other. I try to understand it this way: I can't judge him— I don't have any right to punish or demand anything in return. That would keep myself —and him— stuck in the past. He may have been doing only what he felt forced to do by his own shame or past history. If he had known how, he probably would have done better or differently. Sometimes you know, your mind entraps you, sometimes life feels like a fog. You feel trapped by your past and unable to grow toward your future.

"You don't have the luxury of staring at the past. You can only learn from it and go forward."

"Have you forgiven him?"

"It was hard. There are times when I still struggle with it, you know, when there have been cross words or unreasonable behavior. The truth of the things that happened will always be the truth— they are historical events in my life. They really did take place. To deny that they happened is not living in reality. The greater work, though, the *real* miracle, is in stating the truth of how things were, and taking the path of love and reconciliation.

"You cannot run from the pain in your life. People are always telling you to forget the past and move on, "Cry me a river, build me a bridge and get over it" as the flippant phrase goes. Only people who are numbing themselves to their *own pain* would say a thing like that. There are a lot of people out there running from their pain because people have thrown that phrase around so much, and trying to anesthetize themselves from their pain by buying stuff and working themselves to death. I strongly feel that you have to go back and visit that pain, to grieve it and make peace with it— if only for a time. And *then* bury it, taking what is most useful and full of hope, moving on. The love you find in doing so is great fuel and will give you incredible strength for giving of yourself.

"It is the only way to live your life with courage and strength. I had such dreams that everything would turn out okay in the end.

It *has* turned out okay, but not because *he* changed or my marriage changed. *I* changed. There is no greater truth than this, though:"

"What's that?" asked Jeff.

"I don't care who you are, *you will never be able to afford yourself the luxury of un-forgiveness.* It will rob you of everything you were ever meant to be. It will keep you a prisoner in the darkest coldest prison hole and you will never, *ever,* see the light of a glorious day if you keep the prisoner of your anger hostage. *Set your prisoners free, and you will be set free yourself."*

We were all silent, contemplating the weight of what she just said, and truthfully, probably every one of us sitting there felt perfectly entitled to hold on to our petty past injuries.

"Sometimes I still grieve the loss of what I *could have had*—you know, a happy marriage and all that. For a while, I tried to put back, through 'finding someone' or 'obtaining a goal' what had never been there in the first place. I was trying to heal myself that way. I tried to "make a family"—complete with a loving husband and a positive influence for my children. You know, like a cake mix. I tried desperately, for years, to undo the harm that had been done, to heal myself by spackling the wounds with everything I could think of, like 'staying busy'. But it never would have worked, to try to manufacture a family... so I quit trying. I'm happy with the way things are right now. It is still a struggle, to make ends meet, but you really can find contentment and joy in the simplest of pleasures."

"I don't think I could ever have understood the pain in other people's lives if I hadn't been through hell myself. Look around you carefully— when you're at work, or especially at church. Someone may be going through what I went through, or what you, *yourselves,* go through. That truth alone compels us to reach out to others. I think my children have a greater understanding of the struggles of other people because they have had to struggle so much themselves. Each one of them is a hero, though, truthfully, they don't even know that they are.

"There is nothing worse than being isolated in the midst of your personal tragedy because others are too self-absorbed to take the time to listen. There were so many times I wished someone would have taken me for coffee to ask how I was doing, if they had just reached out. Healing doesn't come instantaneously at an altar—not that it *couldn't*. It usually comes through being able to be real with people who care about you, who will help you sort through how you feel, and love you unconditionally. It's painful to listen to the pain of others, but sharing that pain with them helps see them through their dark night of the soul.

"This is the *real* function of the church— not just loving in words, but in deeds and truth. We— I mean the church— can't be all about *saying* we love others, we have to put our comfort and convenience aside and actually *do* it. Otherwise, it's just a Dog and Pony Show."

"Those are tough words—but they're true." Jeff offered. "Seeing you here week after week, month after month, knowing some of the things you've done and achieved, I *never* would have guessed you went through anything. You just seem to have your act together."

"Yeah, it's all an illusion." she laughed. "But it's true, you know. We never really know what things people go through.

"I have an expression:
You might have gone through hell, but you don't have to hang drapes there!"

We looked at one another for an instant and then everyone laughed heartily.

"If what you're saying is true, then what we're having here every week is really, well, *church*." commented Steve.

Everyone voiced their agreement.

"Hey, I have a question for *you* guys."

She looked about her. "My biggest reservation in telling all of you any of this, is that you would look at me differently from now on. There's a sense of shame in abuse. Besides, I can't let what is in the past color my future— why, *anything* can happen! Please — *promise* me you won't see me any differently from now on? Let's just pretend. It'll be fun! *You'll* see."

Steve took an exaggerated sip of his coffee and set his mug down on the table resolutely.

"Nope." he said. "We can't promise you *that*! I *guarantee* you that we'll never think of you quite the same."

Chapter 13

They say the cat got his tongue, but I think the cat gave it to him.

The first couple of times he came in without a word, and with the exception of introducing himself, and he left without a word. Just a polite nod of excusing himself.

His name was John, and he worked with numbers-lots of them-for an insurance company. That says a lot. I don't work with numbers very well. I don't even socialize with them. John was twenty-eight and had never been married. He usually came at around eight or eight-thirty, and sat quietly in the background. He was about 5'9" and his hair was kinda thinned out on top. He wore glasses and in winter, a hat with ear flaps.

For at least a month, John would come and sit quietly, smiling kindly when I offered him a sweet roll, a muffin, or a crepe, but seldom said a word. Instead, he listened to the more gregarious folk expound on their many viewpoints and drank coffee or tea. In rare instances, he would offer his opinion, and the whole room suddenly became hushed, so unusual it was for him to speak. He spoke gently and with great humility, unlike so many of the other men who came and with great bravado (amid protestations about their spiritual and personal humility) filled the room with their postulates and axioms.

Then, one Saturday night at The Open Door Café, something happened that changed John forever, and it came in the form of a ball of fur.

It was a little gray tabby cat, the runt of a litter of kittens that had been born in our house. Mama White Cat had, shall we say, been somewhat indiscrete in being seen around our little town with Tux (as we named him) a handsome black and white tom that always looked like he was "puttin' on the Ritz". Tux actually looked as if he was wearing a tuxedo, complete with spats. So then, the little gray tabby was a granddaughter cat of Mama White and Tux.

One Saturday night the kitten had overcome some of it's reserve, and was skittering between the feet and legs of every guest between the foyer and the library. I was asking if anyone could hold it since I was afraid it would get under foot. I plopped it down in John's lap and told him he was the kitty sitter for the evening. He acted a bit flustered at first, but as I passed through with a tray of Swedish meatballs, I saw the kitten nestled in the crook of John's arm, asleep— and he was there until the last guest prepared to leave.

"John, I think we can safely say the cat has adopted you. Look, she's been asleep all evening...do you want to take her home?"

He seemed reluctant at first, but later agreed.

The following week, everyone asked John about the cat.

"What did you name her?"

"Well, I thought at first that I would name her Pork Chop. But she looked like the color of snow, so I call her "Snowball"

"John, it's a gray cat." It was Greg, an engineer— all straight lines and numbers, and always so matter of fact.

""Yes, and—?

"Well, you can't just call a gray cat *snowball*"

"Actually, she's just the color of dirty snow. " John corrected.

"If he wants to name it Snowball you oughtta let him. I say Snowball it is!" Exclaimed Cotton.

There was resounding cheer of approval and Snowball became the first mascot of The Open Door Café.

Thereafter, every Saturday night someone would inquire about Snowball's size and her health, whether she was learning her cat manners and especially if John was ready to give her back.

John himself seemed glad to have had the only mascot the cafe ever had and thus began his two-year sojourn with Snowball and the regulars of the Café.

There was another Saturday night that proved to be life changing, and it started with not John, but Jodi. She was an infrequent visitor, but since someone was available to watch her children that particular night, she was able to attend. She came early and made herself busy in the kitchen helping me prepare food while the guests arrived.

"I haven't dated anyone in so long, Caron. I feel like pretty much giving up. It's been eight years since I've really seen anyone. It seems that guys just don't have any substance— they seem so shallow."

"Why do you say that?"

"They seem okay at first, but then when they're confronted with my children, they just take off."

"But Jodi, you have beautiful children. I can't believe they've grown so much-they aren't allowed to make me feel that old!"

"Yes, but most men don't understand…" She looked at me and sat down at the kitchen table. There were tears in her eyes. I sat down too and listened.

"They don't see two beautiful children, Caron. They only see the fact that they are biracial. My children have names. They have feelings and dreams. They aren't a *color*. They're *children*. The relationship I was in was abusive, and I was a prisoner. I became trapped in the relationship and I was threatened into marrying him. The only bright and beautiful thing I have to show for all the pain is the fact that I have my children."

"Jodi, any man who would walk away from you because of your children's skin color isn't worthy of you *or* your children. They need to be confronted about their own fears and bigotry. I can't help but think there is a man out there with a heart big enough for you and your children- big enough for the world to fit inside."

There were tears in her eyes and I could see she had been down this hard road more than once. She was short and with strawberry blonde hair. She was trim and healthy looking, with gray eyes and light freckles.

"It would take a miracle," she returned, almost cynically, with a hardness that betrayed her loss of hope. "It's been eight years, Caron. I think it's hopeless."

"I know it seems that way, but believing that the best is yet to come— well, it has to start somewhere."

Guests started arriving- they just walked right in the front door and some of them came in the dining room, calling greetings and hello's into the kitchen and the study.

The final preparations were made, Jodi asked me if she looked okay. I knew that she meant, 'Do I look like I've been crying?'

"You're just fine." I reassured her.

She smiled a little.

"Can I help with something? Anything?"

"Here, put these on the buffet in the living room.' She took the tray of roll-ups into the living room and a moment later I saw here slip into chair at the dining room table. I only learned afterward how significant the night was.

As she described it, it was all stardust and magic when "he' sat down.

"Who could that be?" (I had been busy in the kitchen most of the evening, and had not seen who was sitting where).

"Don't you *know* him?" she said in whispered tones the next morning at church. She continued, "When he came in, I was thinking to myself '*Who's that*?' Then he sat down right next to me after you got him his coffee! Don't you remember when you brought him a mug from the kitchen? Then when he started talking-he's so articulate. He ponders things before he says them. Afterwards, when people were getting ready to leave, he asked me for my email address."

"Oh! You mean *John*— the quiet guy, glasses? Yeah, he's everybody's favorite."

" Isn't he *wonderful*? And he wrote me the sweetest note—he sent me an email this morning."

"Jodi" I looked at her and she was glowing. "Jodi, he's really a precious guy— I mean, a *really* good guy. Are you serious-I mean, you really are interested?"

"Are you kidding? When he started talking there was just something that...well, I don't know what it is... it gets to me."

"No, really, I think that it's wonderful—he's really a great guy. I just think nobody knows it..."

What I *wanted* to say was that I didn't want anyone to treat him badly, that he deserved the best because he was such a sincere, truly good person— someone you never had to watch your back with

I looked at her, giddy and full of anticipation. "You know, I think you might have discovered the best-kept secret of The Open Door Cafe."

Through the weeks and then the months ahead, John met Jodi's children and grew to love them, not as another race, but as part of the human race. They were, after all, children.

Jodie and John have overcome many hardships on their road and always with unconditional love. They are the kind of couple that blesses me every time I see them.

Maybe both of them had given up hope; maybe they thought they didn't have a prayer. But hope fulfilled is often just around the corner in the most unlikely of places, and it is just as often when we've lost all hope. It sees no failure, no skin color, no limits, and most of all, hope always seeks higher ground.

Chapter 14

Sometimes you just haven't got a prayer. And that's when things *really* start to happen for you.

It was getting kind of late, and it had been a light crowd. Steve and I had been talking in the kitchen for a few minutes— he always liked to help (once, he even did the dishes) and then went into the living room to join the few remaining guests.

In the living room, there were six or seven women who had come from various backgrounds. One was sitting in a wing chair and the others were sitting on the couch. Some of them were from Connersville, Indiana, and had driven a while to get there. The tone seemed somewhat subdued when we entered the room.

He eased into a recliner and asked them how they were. He already had his coffee mug, but I'd forgotten mine and went back into the dining room to get it. As I returned, I could hear him comment, "You don't say... *five* of you are widows?"

I paused at the counter, listening. I knew that the odds of *that* happening were slim, especially since there were so few women there that night to begin with. Moreover, I couldn't have called fifty people and reached five women who had all lost their husbands, much less got them to attend the cafe that night.

I've learned that when something out of the ordinary happens, to pay close attention to what will follow, for the times of unusual-what-are-the-odds-coincidence are times when God shows up and Something Wonderful happens.

I went back into the living room and found a seat on a small footstool. One of them was sharing how her husband had passed away. Vickie was her name. She was a beautiful woman, with ash blonde hair, high cheekbones and expressive eyes. She was soft-spoken and genuinely sweet-natured in addition to being meticulous.

As she continued her story, the front door opened and then closed. I heard heavy footsteps, and before I could turn around to see who it was, a tall fellow came into the living room. It was Mark, an occasional late Saturday visitor to the cafe.

He slumped down in a chair. It seemed so exaggerated that it was almost comical, and broke the solemn atmosphere. He was tall and had a playful Southern-ness about him— a country boy, although he had grown up in Ohio. He was matter of fact and good at sizing people up. He was also an entrepreneur at heart, and a born promotion man. He had been helping promote gospel concerts for a long time.

"I've had it!" he exclaimed, running his hand through his thick head of dark hair. He looked like a wild man, sitting in the graceful white wing chair.

"What happened to *you*?" I asked, laughing.

"I've just been to another "Single's Function"— at a church."

"You mean there are *other* singles' groups out there?" Steve asked wryly..

"Can I get you a mug of coffee? You can tell us all about it."

"Sure—you know how I take it, don't you?"

"You cut me to the quick, sir." I mocked in a fake British accent.

"Now, what the heck was I thinkin'? Anyway, I was gonna come here first, but someone called me up and invited me to go to this thing at their church. We were sitting there talking to a couple of women, and when the friend of the one I was talking to got up to use the restroom, the one I was talking to put her hand on my leg under the table!"

"At a *church*?"

"Well, I guess not everyone who goes there is a Christian— anyway, I knew I'd better leave or I'd end up some place I didn't want to be. So I came here as fast as I could."

"Well, you did the right thing." kidded one of the women sitting on the couch.

"I'm so sick of going to single's groups! I've been goin' to these things for ten years, and I've never met anybody."

"Is that why you're going to them?"

"Isn't that why everybody does?"

"No, maybe not everybody. Some of us just want to be with some other people who can relate to where we're coming from."

"Well, this is the only place I can think of that's like this—there isn't any other single's group like this one."

He took a drink of his coffee and then rested the mug on his knee. "The trouble is, I just don't fit in with anybody."

"We think you fit in just fine, huh Caron?" affirmed Steve.

"No! I mean with women. I'm either too worldly for the spiritual, churchy types, or too churchy for the worldly ones."

"I'm sure that there's *someone* out there who would be willing to accept you just the way you are. Why don't you just forget about meeting someone and just be friends with everyone?" I said. "You know, we were just having a discussion before you came in. You want to hear something strange?"

"That's what I intend to do." He then added, "What's strange?"

"With one exception, every woman sitting on the couch has been widowed. The really odd part is that they're the only women who came tonight. We were just listening to each of their stories when you came in."

"Wow. That kinda makes my problem seem kinda petty, doesn't it?"

"Well, your problem is important to *you*. It's just that other people have different problems." I didn't want him to feel like I was minimizing his situation.

"Vickie was just telling her story." interjected Steve.

"Oh, wait, Mark. I should have introduced you to everyone." I apologized. "I forgot you didn't know everyone here."

I went around the group and introduced them all. Mark shook hands with all the ladies (he already knew Steve).

Vickie continued her story and I took some plates into the kitchen and started putting food away. I then ran some water into the sink and added detergent. I had never minded doing the dishes, even though there was no dishwasher in my tiny kitchen—after all, if I didn't have the Open Door Cafe, there wouldn't *be* any extra dishes to wash. I was halfway done with the dessert plates and the saucers when Steve came in holding the fifty-cup coffee urn.

"This is empty. Did you want to make more?"

"Do you think anyone will drink any more? It's kinda late."

"Probably not— I'll bring the rest of the cups in."

I finished all the dishes and Steve came into the dining room just as I was straightening the chairs and sat down. I sat down as well, and we talked about the evening.— He would often stay a little later and we, sometimes with Cotton, would talk about ways to make the Open Door Cafe better, what was making it work, what wouldn't work. Sometimes we prayed for the folks who came there and sometimes we even prayed for one another. Cotton had left earlier than usual because he had been hiking at the state park earlier that day. Both of us thought it was odd that most of the women that night were widows.

Mark and Vickie had been standing in the hallway for some time talking. It seems the others from Connersville had left; though they were waiting for Vickie out in the car. At length, we heard the front door close and a moment later Mark dashed into the dining room and slid into a seat.

"Look—she gave me her number!" he held up a small folded piece of paper triumphantly. "I hope you don't mind— we tore it out of your guest book, Caron."

I sighed heavily, and then tongue in cheek, I added, "I *guess*... The sacrifices I make for you guys..."

"Mark, you act like you've never gotten a woman's phone number." Steve was smiling.

"Not hers! Isn't she *somethin'*?" Mark drawled. He was on cloud nine.

"She sure is."

"Did you see her smile?" Mark grinned from ear to ear.

"See, Mark. It's not really as hopeless as you thought it was." Steve assured him.

Mark continued to sit with us for awhile and we prayed together before he and Steve got up to leave.

It was several weeks later that I saw Mark again.

It was really warm outside. No, it was *steamy*—just as it always is in the Ohio River basin in July—and a large single's group from a HUGE church in Cincinnati came. I had gone through two urns of coffee and was rummaging through my cabinets looking for desserts I could make relatively quickly. I always kept things on hand that could be thrown together artfully in a situation like this, but there were so many people there I envisioned pouring Cheerios into a bowl as a last resort. It was the largest turnout to date— thirty two. I found that night that large numbers make your ego feel great, but you sacrifice a lot of intimacy and ambiance because the sheer numbers make it hard to function. It's usually so loud that close conversation and sharing seem almost impossible.

As I made my way into the dining room from the kitchen with yet another urn of coffee, it was necessary to squeeze between guests engaged in conversation. I don't have a loud voice to begin with, so it was hard to get through. Finally I reached the armoire where I had the coffee supplies. I was plugging in the coffee urn when someone called my name from behind me.

In the sea of faces, I could make out Mark's face and then Vickie's. Then I saw the most amazing thing. Right in front of my face appeared a lovely hand from nowhere—with a sparkling engagement ring on it! Everyone cheered and hugged them. They were both beaming.

They had both been single for a long time— Mark for about ten years— and Vickie for seven. For some weird reason, they had not, for all those previous months of the cafe, ever come on the same night. Mark seldom came at all, and when he did, it was usually after the folks from Connersville had already left.

Vickie and Mark got married about six months later, in Connersville, on November twenty-fifth. Cotton was my escort, and I wouldn't have missed it for anything. Oh, in case you're wondering, Cotton behaved himself and was quite gentlemanly. The wedding was Saturday evening, so I had to get back in time for the coffee house.

To my surprise, Mark and Vickie actually made an appearance at the coffee house on their way to where they spent their honeymoon, the Golden Lamb! Mark said that since they met at my house they thought it would be only fitting to stay at the 'Lamb only four blocks away. It was a beautiful sight to see their glowing faces, Vickie still in her lovely wedding dress, and Mark looking as if he walked off with a treasure.

They are happily married to this day and love to tell *everyone* about how they met one Saturday night, when Mark had finally given up, at the Open Door Cafe.

Chapter 15

Of course, *some* folk do not believe in such things.

But what you are about to read here is the absolute truth. For those of a doubtful nature, I will let you draw what conclusion you will. For the rest of you— some of whom may have had your *own* experience, what you are about to read may seem strange (certainly no less strange than I feel even in the telling of it). Yet it may encourage you to press on, to endure hardship and to overcome your darkest fears...of failure, of abandonment, of fears unknown.

It was on a late May evening, when I was ready to give up on a dream, that a dreamlike visit, just in the nick of time, assured me that I was not failing, that I was not abandoned, and that even unnamed fears can be laid to rest.

A small shop had become available behind The Golden Lamb Inn just two months before. It was cozy and quaint, a barn red frame house with tan trim and lots of charm. It was, in fact, owned by The Golden Lamb and at the time I was in a position to rent it.

Several fearful and timid people had been concerned that I held The Open Door Café in my home, and had encouraged me to try to find another place to hostess it in. They didn't, however, offer any ideas as to how I would *pay* for such a thing. I would have to be the underwriter of such a venture. There was no budget through my church at the time for my ministry, and that is true of many single's ministries in churches

Since everything seemed to fall into place as far as the timing, amount of rent, etc., it seemed only natural that I should try to make a go of it moving the café off site.   After moving lots of furniture down to the little shop that was no more than four blocks from my house, I decided that it would be a good idea also to open the café on Friday nights as well as the usual Saturday night. To come out even, I had to have twenty-one guests every Friday and every Saturday. I consistently got twenty to twenty-five people on a Saturday night, so it really seemed possible. If it became self-supporting, it wouldn't be necessary for me to support it myself— a single mother.

At the time, I was working for a heating and cooling company and was able to supplement the rent with my own income. This was soon to change, for after I agreed to rent the building, it was found that since two of our major clients (Drug Emporium and Kmart) had filed various forms of bankruptcy, and that I would be downsized out. This would be the case even though my *projected* sales looked very promising. It later turned out that *all* of my prospective clients signed contracts with my employer when their contracts were up for re-negotiation. The result was that when the other clients were no longer viable, there were new ones to take their place. This, of course, did me no good, as I was no longer with the company. In the meantime, though, it seemed that the best thing to do was to try to make the café work— at least until I was able to find another position.

The little shop had, before I rented it, been a golf outfitter with everything for the golfing enthusiast. Why, there was even a putting green in a small space where the brick walkway formed right angles with a sidewalk. Instead of grass, the putting green was constructed of green felt held in place by what looked like huge wreath pins.

I went to the café as usual that Friday night and brewed the coffee, laid out pound cake and strawberries, cookies and a fruit tray for any prospective guests.

But an hour went by and no one came. An hour and a half after that, and still no one showed up. This was odd. There was always at least *someone* there on a Friday.

I don't know if I was disappointed or disgusted. Just as I had done on Saturday nights when the café was at my house, I had to prepare desserts, etc. just *in case* people came; but I never really knew if it would be one person or twenty— or in this case, none. The same was true on a Saturday night when I held the café at my home, but not as much was at stake. I could always freeze what I didn't use. The shop had no refrigerator so I would have to transport everything in my car.

I had also purchased trays of annuals the day before— petunias and begonias— for the little kidney-shaped flowerbed that had been the putting green. A few days before, I had removed the felt of the putting green and prepared the soil for flowers. The bed was freshly dug and fertilized, and since it appeared that no one would be attending the cafe that night I changed back into my blue jeans and set about the planting of all those little seedlings.

As I turned the tender little plants out of their plastic trays, one by one by one, I wrestled with the whole café thing. I thought of the desserts on the table inside that no one would eat, of the coffee I must throw away. I wondered why I was even planting the flowers. I wondered why, every time I took a bold step forward, trying to bring about the thirty, sixty and one-hundred fold, as the gospel proverb admonished, trying to devote more of my time, energy, talent and gifts to accomplish greater good, everything seemed to go wrong— especially with my job.

Did it always have to come down to this? Was I only being foolish, or was it really a spiritual battle? Should I give up and admit defeat, or persevere through my hardships? How do I know when to give up and when to press on? When does determination turn into foolhardiness? Did everyone who ever did anything extraordinary question their own sanity (like everyone else around them questioned it)? Why could no one ever seem to answer my questions?

Playing devil's advocate with myself, I tried to err on the side of having faith, always trying to bear fruit. Whatever questions arose, when in doubt I chose to press on. I'd read of famous inventors, men and women with great dreams of accomplishing great good, who were ready to give up, yet didn't. Of how Alexander Graham Bell tried to sell his improvements of the telephone to Western Union but was turned down— which led to the formation of AT&T. How Colonel Sanders took his recipe for fried chicken to over a thousand companies before someone made him a millionaire in his mid-sixties. Of how F. W. Woolworth's family thought him mad and wanted to have him committed because he dreamed of a "chain" of dime stores that would span the country— rather than the traditional and safe hometown five-and-dime. And most folks know that the man who held the worlds record for *strike-outs* was, in fact, the great "Babe" Ruth. Failure is ALWAYS part of success, and often you learn so much more from a mistake than a triumph. You never have cozy without cold and miserable. You never have the glorious sun without the dark night of the soul.

These men and women of courage never let the lack of imagination on the part of others, those in the vast crowds of ordinary people, shatter their dreams. I didn't want to stand before God one day and hear that I fell short of a miracle because I gave up too soon, or was concerned that people around me didn't understand what I "had to do". And even more crucial was the urgency of replacing my flawed, selfish, shortsighted dreams with His eternal, untarnished dreams through me. I wanted so to be His hands, His smile, His comfort, and His feet.

What *really* bothered me, though, was that I realized how many comfortable Christians, many of whom were sitting in the same row with me at church, who didn't want to do *anything* remarkable for God, who were comfortable with a timecard Christianity, putting in the required amount of time and then going home to their other priorities. They led lives of duty and obedience, never doing more than what was required. They didn't have any dreams of doing something dazzling that would make God smile.

But I wanted more. I really *meant* the words to the songs I was singing on Sunday mornings. After all, why sing the songs, going through the motions, if I didn't *mean* it? I really longed to make up for years I had squandered on my own interests and hobbies, on my own interior world. I wanted to make my remaining years on this earth count for something.

I knew from the experience of hosting the café in my home, that there was *nothing* to be compared with walking in the gifts and talents that God placed in you. Let me put it this way:

There is nothing you could ever desire that will give you as much fulfillment as exercising your God-given and ordained gifts, and fulfilling your destiny.

You may run from what people call the 'Call of God' your whole life, all because you misunderstand in the first place what it is He would have you do. You *think* He's going to "make" you be a missionary. He doesn't *make* you do anything. *But you may find you have the desire to do something that you have never had before.* Something becomes a consuming passion.

He wants you to give your passions to Him. He lives in our bright dreams and our passions, He is alive in the beautiful things we create, because He is the Creator; He lives in the kind acts of caring for the needs of others— because He cares for our needs, practical as they are. He dwells in the repair of a car, the well-baked cake, the carefully constructed bridge and the jazz ensemble that sings to your soul. He is in unseen kindnesses, and the candy bar left on someone's desk at work, He is in the eyelashes of a newborn girl and in the smile on her mouth. He created the passions and dreams in you before you were born. Did you ever wonder *why* you love to decorate? Look at how He decorates the night sky and places the mountains just so— look at how the late afternoon sun on Christmas Day gleams on the rolling snowy hills and falls across the wall and table top there. Just take a look up at the clouds, how, parted and full of night they lay just below the moon so that their shadows and curves frame the crescent and the stars and the galaxies beyond.

When your dreams are aligned with His purpose, *you are traveling together on the same highway*, accomplishing the same goal, and it becomes effortless to work within your passions. Things that would weary other folk— or try their patience— are like play for you, because it is what you were *designed* to do. Why? Because you are doing what you were always *meant* to do. It's child's play for grownups.

There were times when guests on a Saturday night would comment "*I'd* go to using paper plates and Styrofoam cups if *I* were *you*." Or, "There's no way *I'd* wash all those cups and saucers if I were you."

I would smile and protest that I could *never* do that. How could I explain that each cup, each saucer, each dessert plate and knife and fork and serving tray only served all the more to confirm that I was walking right smack in the middle of the destiny He called me to? Each washed teaspoon, each espresso cup was an expression of praise, and when I washed them, I was holding in my hands all the hope and love they represented.

"I was made for this." I would think, holding the cream pitcher with bubbles cascading down the side into the hot water. All this time, I thought that ministry was in the sermon, in the talking, even in a musical ministry. Ministry is in those things, but now I see it is in all our acts filled with Him. My ministry is in the warmth of the coffee cup in someone's hands, the sudden laughter in the next room, in the warm embrace of those I've grown to love, and in their smile upon entering my hallway and everyone greeting them by name.

How bitter, then, were my thoughts of failure as I rose with dirty knees from that flowerbed, wondering if I had jumped the gun, wondering if any of what I had dared to do mattered.

You who are reading this may never know the anguish of one of your fellow human beings who longs to do something heroic and wonderful for the good of many, but can't because they need a little help to do so. And it might be help from you! Think of it. They have the desire but not the means, and you have the means, but no desire. Imagine what could happen if the two of you got *together...* We must never refuse help to someone when it is within our power to do so. It is one of the great sins. You may never be aware of it, but God may have brought you across their path at just the right time for that very purpose.

Since there was no garden hose, I had to use a bucket to water in the seedlings. I estimated five or six buckets-full of water to soak them in good. But by trip number *eleven* to the water spigot, I was pretty tired of watering the flowers in.

I came eventually to one conclusion— that even if no one *ever again* stepped across the threshold of that coffee house that my labor would be sown to the heavens and that my reward may never even *be* on this earth. It was His coffeehouse, and if He was the only guest I had, then that was just fine with me. That is how I resolved it in my own mind— that as long as God was pleased with my life's labor, nothing else really mattered, and that eventually there would be some good to come of it, even if it was only in the life to come.

The evening was perfect in temperature, warm and dry for mid-May in Ohio. The setting sun lit up the new green leaves and fell between the branches in golden bars that washed across the grasses in chartreuse and verdant emerald. A small swarm of gnats danced for sheer joy, a dizzying ballet of up and down rhythm in the brilliant golden glow. I paused there, wondering if heaven held May evenings and first snowfalls, and sunlight like golden waterfalls.

This was pretty close to heaven.

I leaned forward to turn on the spigot and looked up absently at nothing in particular. But something stole my attention. It was a truck, which slowly rounded the corner and came into view from behind the southwest corner of the frame house. It was no ordinary truck. It was a *pristine* vintage seafoam green pickup with ivory sidewall tires and an ivory sidewall spare mounted just above the passenger side bumper. I'm guessing late 1940's to early '50's. I *immediately* thought of a pickup truck in an illustration that appeared in a Dick, Jane and Sally reader I had in the second grade, where they visited their uncle's farm. What an idyllic existence they seemed to have there on the farm— as if nothing bad could happen in the world of Dick, Jane and Sally. Where everything was a happy dog named Spot, and an orange cat named Puff. I had remembered the truck often—any time I thought of the beginning reading workbooks we had used. I had even looked for a model of an early '50's pickup truck.

I have to say here that I love vintage *anything*, and have a special fondness for vintage vehicles. I used to assemble models with my son when he was little. I had once dated a mechanic who restored old Corvettes and went to quite a few car shows, cruise-ins and swap meets. He had a fifty-eight Corvette, red with the convertible hard top and white coves. We used to tool around in it. I was always amazed at how loud the engine sounded, and I wondered if it was *supposed* to be that loud, or if it was just old. Of course, I never asked him, but later I noticed that all the old cars and trucks sounded the same.

Inside the truck were two people I could barely see. I wanted to give them a thumbs up because the truck was in absolutely cream puff condition.— but they had already passed the point where they could see me. I looked down at the level of water in the bucket and up again to get one more look at the truck before it was out of sight.

Wait— it was turning into the parking lot of The Golden Lamb!

"Great!" I thought. *"I'll just wait until they go inside and then I'll go check it out."*

I turned off the water and hefted the bucket once more, starting toward the flowerbed. Sixty-seven steps from where the faucet was to where the flower bed lay. I slowly soaked the last of the seedlings and plucked a remaining little weed from the spongy dark earth.

I stood up, and something caught my attention directly to the right of me. The green pickup had circled through the parking lot, which was comprised of two sections, and was pulling slowly into a parking spot right in front of the café which shared some of the parking spots! I didn't mean to be rude, but I couldn't help but stare.

The passengers, a man and a woman, opened their doors and got out. They were smiling and looked at one another and then the man came around the rear of the truck and they started toward me. I peeled off my wet leather gardening gloves and rubbed my hands together trying to dry them, but ended up wiping them on my jeans. I was a mess and now I had company.

There was something odd, but not unpleasant, about them– in their dress as well as their demeanor. They were two of the most perfect people I've ever seen. Time seemed to freeze in the moment they walked from the truck to where I stood in front of the door. They seemed out of place— no, that's not it.

It was more like they suddenly were *in* place, and everything *else* around them was *not-quite-right*.

It was a distinct shift in perspective, like a figure/ground drawing: like the classic black and white silhouette of a vase that could also be two opposing faces looking at one another.

It wasn't anything you could define and say "*That's* it". It was just a different feeling than you get from ordinary people. It was not in what they were, but in what they *weren't*. It was not in what they said, but in what was *not* said. They looked about them as if everything they looked at was new to them, even the most ordinary of things, from the bucket, to the trowel, to the brick of the walkway.

"*They must not be from around here. Maybe they're foreign.*" I at first thought to myself.

They were dressed oddly— not like the people I was used to seeing at swap meets and car shows— or even at the cafe for that matter. They were in their mid-thirties, I guessed, but something seemed just, well, *off*. Their skin, youthful in appearance, was betrayed by the crow's feet at the corners of their eyes. They projected wisdom beyond their years, of great and gentle hearts, possessing a certain depth and largeness that comes from being *remarkably old*. They just didn't *look* old. I remember thinking, "*I want their secret.*"

She was adorable, in a housedress with a small floral pattern. Just the sort of print that I would have picked from a bolt of new spring fabric at the general store. Her hair was a natural golden color and braided in a single long thick braid, which hung down her back I could only imagine how long it was when it was not braided. I don't think she had any makeup on, but her face was pure and sweet and innocent, in perfect proportions, like the faces of my daughters.

He wore a straw hat with a wide fabric band, and a *bow tie*. Oh, yes—and *suspenders*. And it was strange how it seemed he was used to wearing such clothes, and, in fact, as if he *always* did. His muted tan plaid shirt was short-sleeved and he had on tan trousers. Neither he nor she was very tall. They would have looked perfectly at home back in nineteen and forty-five, coming from a church supper back home to a little farm in Indiana

Back *then*.

I smiled and said hello, offering my hand across the flowerbed— but suddenly aware I was extending a damp and somewhat muddy hand, I murmured an awkward apology. Here were guests to my café, and I was so unprepared—I felt self-conscious in my jeans with dirty knees and tennis shoes and my tank top.

"We saw your sign from far away..." she continued. "This is a—"

"It's a Christian Coffee House..."

"We *thought* so! Didn't we?" She glanced at her partner, who only smiled slightly.

"Welcome!" I offered. "I was just—" I rubbed my right hand on my jeans.

She extended her hand, simultaneously stepping over the shovel and the hard rake— without even looking down. "It's all right— really, we don't mind." she said and shook my wet hand. She looked to her partner then added, "May we come in?"

"Of course you can!" I laughed. "I wasn't actually expecting anyone to come as it was getting so late, but I'm glad you're here.

Believe it or not, on Saturday nights there are actually people here. If you come in, I'll give you the nickel tour."

They walked on past me, without hesitating a wit, and it was I who ended up following *them*. They seemed to know the way, and walked up the steps, opening the door to the enclosed porch where little navy blue and white checked café curtains hung on cheerful brass rods. White ceramic tile-topped tables sported candles whose flames danced within glass globes. Even the floor was a giant checkerboard of deep navy and off white tile. I was tagging along behind them—great tour guide *I* was. They looked about them with great interest, but not at what you would think. They seemed intrigued with doorknobs and woodwork, with the carpet (a generic indoor/outdoor type), and wall switches, the fabric of the tablecloth.

Then, through the French doors they walked, to the largest room. It was painted a deep copper and there were various shapes of tables with white tablecloths and vases with fresh flowers. Several paintings, including some prints by Maxfield Parrish, one of my favorite artists, graced the walls. The armoire from my house stood in the corner and near it the odd little corner chair with its burgundy-colored cushion.

On through the café they made their way, leading me. Every room had it's own personality—there were five rooms in all, and each one was cozy and inviting.

They looked from side to side, at the crown molding and the lace curtained windows, the Victorian lamps and the pound cake, noting every detail but saying nothing. It seemed as if they were listening to something I couldn't hear, distracted by something else going on at the same time, *in parallel*, as our silent tour through the café. Thoughtfully he touched the spoons fanned out in a line on the buffet table, and she touched the cut glass pitcher of pink lemonade, then the glasses in the same thoughtful manner as he. You'd think they never *saw* that stuff before.

There was a copy of the article on the singles' coffeehouse lying on a table, and I picked it up. I was timid to even say anything, because they seemed so engrossed in the surroundings.

'This was an article that appeared in a national magazine— about the café. It's just for singles—the café that is. Several people have gotten married who met here. Would you like some fruit—maybe a little piece of cake?"

She seemed lost in thought, but then distracted by my words, looked from the furnishings to my face, refocusing her attention.

"Oh. I don't think I could *eat* anything—could you?" She looked at her partner.

He shook his head ever so slightly. His eyes always seemed to be smiling, even though his face was straight. He had pale blue eyes and a neat moustache. I couldn't get over how *young* they looked, even with the soft crows' feet.

"*What in the world is going on here, anyway?*" I wondered so loud I was surprised they couldn't hear me. It was just plain old weird.

Most people their age (I couldn't even hazard a guess) just wouldn't dress the way they were dressed. They didn't sound as if they were from another country. Maybe it was another dimension.

As they passed me by, and with a bright window beyond the man, I studied the fabric of his shirt in the bright light, expecting telltale signs of a thrift shop, expecting, perhaps, some frayed edges from having been pressed too much, or a loose thread hanging from a button. But it looked like a brand new shirt.

Writing of it now, *I don't even know why it occurred to me to look for signs of wear, and I remember thinking to myself at the time, "See if you can tell if his shirt really* is *old.'*—except something was just plain odd and I was looking for clues. *I don't know why I instinctively tried to look for clues as to their age or authenticity.* It was as if I was dreaming and in my dream trying to determine if it was only a dream by reasoning certain things.

Let me try to explain it this way:

You could walk through a crowded mall, with *hundreds* of people, and these two would stand out.

You would know they were unusual, but you wouldn't be able to define *why* they were unusual. You would just know, without knowing *how* you knew.

I wanted to ask them what was up. Something was going on, I could just feel it. I expected a joke of some kind, expected them to be the leaders of a gigantic singles' group and that any moment they would call out, "Okay, guys, everybody in!"

"There are more rooms back here." I offered. I led them to the last room, the window of which faced the parking lot and the green truck. It was a huge window with lots of windowpanes. My hammered dulcimer was in front of the window as was a Tiffany lamp that served as cheap advertising for the cafe to patrons of the nearby restaurant.

"You play this?" She asked. She lightly fingered the strings.

"Yes." I smiled. "It's a hammered dulcimer. I usually play traditional Irish music- I haven't mastered praise music yet— everything I play turns into Irish tunes."

"I've heard one before, long ago."

"Then you know how pretty—"

She didn't wait for the remainder of the sentence. She turned to him and said quietly, almost wistfully, "*He's* here—you can feel it, can't you?" She was nodding slightly and he smiled in his eyes, assuring me, he himself nodding, ever so slightly. He looked at me, studying my face.

It was all I could do to keep from asking them, well— you know.

There was such a peaceful feeling, not the feeling you usually get in the presence of complete strangers. She then turned to me, smiling softly and began to speak, as if she was translating, listening as she was talking, listening for what I could not hear.

"This is going to be big. *Really* big." she frowned a little, as if trying to form her words just right. "Listen to me." She smiled. "This—" She glanced about her and then looked intently into my eyes. "This is just the beginning. I know you feel discouraged— and you want to give up, but God will remember that you've been faithful with what He gave you. You have a gift for this. You've done well— His presence is really here. Listen to me. I know you want to give up. But many people are going to be blessed because of what you're doing…"

I suddenly felt so relieved. Relieved that I didn't have to express something that I had spent the previous three hours wrestling with and which filled me with so much confusion and wondering. Hope returned where feelings of failure had been lurking. There were grateful tears welling up on my eyes.

"I'm sorry." I faltered. "I'm just so glad you understand. I thought you would think that because no one was here that—" Suddenly, it didn't matter at all that no one was there. In fact, it was more fitting that there *wasn't* a soul at the cafe that night— *there wasn't supposed to be.*

She looked at her companion. He really was smiling now, a smile that warmed his face. She turned back to me. "You see, it really isn't about *this* place— what you're doing goes far *beyond* this place. This is only part of something bigger that's yet to come."

There were tears slipping down my cheeks and I wiped them away. I looked at her and then at him. There was strangely no emotion coming from either of them—as if they were oblivious to my reaction.

There was a Knowing-Without-Words of what I was asking in my mind and in my spirit—the overwhelming query. They knew— especially him— and I knew. I just couldn't bring myself to say it.

He was smiling, but acted as if it was time to go, and turned. She followed as they retraced their steps back through the rooms to the front door of the café.

They didn't say Word One as they headed toward the truck, which struck me as a little strange, especially after what had taken place. You know, how you'll usually make small talk in a situation where you're winding down a conversation with total strangers? It just didn't happen.

Outside, she turned around once to smile at me and then got into the truck. They backed up a little and she waved, smiling as he did.

I waved in return, and mouthed, "Thank you."

Slowly they backed out of the parking space as the sun dipped below the houses and trees: and the day closed on that perfect warm spring evening, when the gnats danced in the sunlight, and the primal urgency of spring and new life, new expectations of something wonderful on the horizon hung in the air with the lilacs' heady fragrance. Turning, I stooped and picked up the shovel and pulled a plastic planting instruction insert from the flowerbed.

Then like a lightning bolt, stood upright and looked about. A single, instantaneous, incredible realization of something unnamed and incongruous to the entire scene was flooding my entire consciousness. The very Answer to my unvoiced Question was in an instant realization— the type of realization that, in a dream, convinces you that it *is* a dream by its irrational nature— something like, 'This has to be a dream- the dog *can't* be talking because dogs don't talk in real life'.

My eyes searched the lot where the truck, visible only seconds before, had now disappeared. From where I was standing, I was able to look across the entire parking lot, up *and* down Main Street for blocks, and *also* up and down Sycamore Street—four street directions, including the parking lot.

Nothing.

The realization, so striking it was nearly a tangible thing, filled the lot and the café and the air surrounding me, like the electricity of a dark thunderstorm:

The vintage green pickup truck, without a mark or smudge, with the glorious white sidewall tires and brilliant chrome bumpers— the happy green truck with the pleasant man and the adorable being with her fair blonde hair braided down her back— made no noise.

*An interesting footnote:

This evening, after I finished writing this, the mother of one of my youngest daughter's friends called and said that she had an extra ticket to see "A Christmas Carol" at the Playhouse in the Park in Cincinnati. I had just enough time to get ready.

Once we were there, we waited in the lobby until it was time to be seated. She asked me how the book was going and I said fine, though I didn't give her any details. I told her I never dreamed that people would love the Open Door Cafe or that it would have the positive impact that it had on people's lives. She agreed. I was wondering if I should tell her about the chapter I had written that day, this chapter, then decided she would probably think I was crazy, making it up, etc, etc. I was debating internally when she said, "Caron, have you ever wondered if maybe, well, *angels* came to your coffee house?"

WHAT?

What would motivate her to say that, just when I was debating whether I should tell her the subject matter of the chapter I had just finished writing just two and a half hours before? Nobody said anything about angels. Not even close. Was it a confirming word, an affirmation of what had, indeed, happened? It was just one of those little amazing "coincidences" that seem to be happening all the time— signposts along the way, perhaps?)

Chapter 16

It's all in the cattail bouquet. Allow me to explain.

Lots of people have asked me, "So... did *you* meet someone at 'The Open Door Cafe'?" Maybe you even wondered it yourself.

Once, in a prayer group, we had to split into small groups and we were instructed to share from our heart some areas where we needed prayer.

I was in a group with a couple of men. Just my luck. Why couldn't I have sat with some of the gals? How could I bring it up? They'll think I'm a comedienne.

One of them requested prayer for a move he was contemplating. He had a family, which included at least one adolescent who would have to start over at a new high school.

The other fellow had a step-father who was diagnosed with a life-threatening illness and he wanted to be reconciled with him.

Finally it came to my turn.

"How do you know if someone is "the One" for you?"

They both smiled.

The first one answered, "Well, if he's committed to his own personal growth and you truly love each other... Why— is there someone you're talking to?"

"Well. Not exactly. No, kind of.. the thing is, I have a fleece."

"As in, *'Gideon's* fleece'?"

"Yes."

"What is it— if you don't mind me asking."

"It's cat tails."

Hans winced.

"No! Not from a real *live* cat, silly! You know. The ones that grow by the side of the road— and in ponds and swamps and stuff. With the fuzzy tops on 'em?"

"Oh..." They were both grinning and leaned forward just a little.

"And why cattails?"

"Well, for some girls, it's diamonds, and for some girls it's pearls. Now, I like pearls a lot—they're my birthstone. But cattails— well, they just kinda say it all."

"How's that?" They were getting a kick out of this, but I didn't see any point to pretending to be Ice Princess Barbie or anything. I've always been a pretty transparent woman. You may as well lay it all out on the line.

"Well, they're kind of like the Holy Grail, don't you think? After all, the guy who gets me will have to go to a little trouble—you know, "get his feet wet" a little. It's like a quest—for a knight—in a way. *Any* woman would want diamonds. But I'm not just any woman. Cattails may *seem* ordinary—they grow most everywhere. That's why people pass them up all the time. They're really very special, though and not everyone understands that. Sometimes you overlook the most amazing things, thinking they are just ordinary."

"Hey, did you know that when they're 'ripe' you can tap in the top of 'em and they blow up? It's really kind of fun."

"They *do?* I didn't know that. All the *more* reason for a guy to give me cattails. I've always wanted some cattails to put in a crock by the door or on the porch. I asked three or four guys I've dated if they would get me some sometime, and they always say okay— *but they never do.* Do you know why? Because only "the one" for me will—*can*— give them to me. It's like the legend of King Arthur—how no one but Arthur could draw Excalibur from the magic stone. Anyway, one of them was recent.

"He said they grew by the corner where he always got stopped by the traffic light.

"'Is there a way you could pull over and cut some?' I asked him.

"'All you really need is a pocket knife— or some pruning shears.'" I said.

"'Hey, no problem.'" he said.

"I'm still waiting for them.

"He *wanted* to, but he just *didn't* 'for some reason'. Summer came and went, and on into the autumn. He said recently, 'I wanted to give you cat tails, but for some reason— I can't figure out why, I just haven't. I don't get it.'

"You know why, guys? Because I'm not gonna get cat tails from *anyone* but the guy who is willing to bring me the cat tail trophy from the dragon infested lair of the dark, dank and dangerous Swamp of Doom. Even if the guy *knows* it's my fleece, it doesn't seem to make any difference. Of course, not *anyone* can get cattails for me. I mean, it's gotta be from someone I love, too, not just a guy off the street or something..."

They really got a kick out of it. From that point on, both of them would occasionally ask me if I got any cattails. Passing me in the hall, their salutation was, "Cattails?"

"Nope, I'm still waitin'—but when I *do* ... well, you'll be the first to know." Everyone else looked at us as if we were wing nuts. Okay, maybe we were nuts.

It's a great romantic story, this story God is telling. The people in it are just ordinary, but the story, and their realization of the tremendous good that would come of it, is profound and extraordinary. He uses things like cattails and coffee to do something kinda wonderful.

For the longest time, I had a hard time working on this book. Why? Because I didn't know the *end* of the story. There seemed to be so many mysteries and unanswered questions. I felt in some way that I would lack credibility if I didn't have all the answers tied up in a neat little package for you, the reader. How could I tell people to take a leap of faith that I don't quite understand myself?

(Some of you are thinking "That's why they *call* it a leap of *faith..)*

So... I decided to just let God tell this story, mysteries and all. It really is a great love story— and He uses the likes of you and me. It's a story worth telling again and again.

The right one, well, his heart will hear what all of this is saying. And he'll be on a mission—neither hell nor high water will stand between him and those cattails. And when he does bring me cattails, he may just as well be riding a white steed and a broadsword forged in Camelot itself. At least, that's the way *I'll* see him. He'll have to overcome perils, to be sure; most of the fearsome creatures are right there in one's own heart. But you gotta admit, it does make a great love story.

And when I *do* get my cattails, why, *you'll* be the first to know!

Chapter 17

When things didn't work out in the little red building behind The Golden Lamb Inn, I gave most of the furniture that was in it to a single mom with five children whom I worked with. She had come out of a relationship full of turmoil and abuse and needed a fresh start. I gave her dishes, the armoire, wing chairs and a dining room table, a coffee table, a microwave cart, a desk and chair, and framed pictures. I brought the remainder of the furniture home and worked it into the furnishings I already had.

For some weird reason, I always have more furniture than I need. It just finds me and I give it away. Then I get more. What's *up* with that, anyway?

It was July, and it was hot and steamy.

For several weeks I did nothing. I was really discouraged over what I viewed as a "failure" and contemplated what was to come. I wasn't sure if I should continue to host the Open Door Cafe— in my house or otherwise.

I had been reading selections from Oswald Chamber's book, *My Utmost for His Highest*, and one of the devotionals dealt with how Moses had slain an Egyptian. Moses knew his calling was to deliver the Jewish people from slavery. However, in his exuberance to fulfill the plan of God, he took matters into his own hands; and when he killed an Egyptian who was beating one of the Jewish slaves, he set himself back forty years as a result. He dwelt in the wilderness, herding sheep for a living.

Had I taken matters into my own hands as well? Only time would answer my question. All I knew was that I wanted to really know that God was leading me in the next venture, whatever *that* was, and *if* there was even to *be* another venture.

Late at night I would be messing around with different graphic things, mostly designing business cards I had no use for and brochures. I would look through collections of graphic images I had on some discs and I experimented with different special effects and that sort of thing.

That's when the "still, small voice" started bugging me.

"You know, you really *could* be working on the book now, instead of just playing around." The Voice said.

"*Nope.*" I thought. "*I'm done jumping the gun. If God wants me to write a book about the cafe, then He's just going to have to tell me Himself.*"

Now, months before—in February, I think, before I had even *thought* of renting the little red frame building, I had been thinking of how the cafe story would make a wonderful book. It was a *good story*— it had true love, sacrifice, menace and humor; *and,* it might even inspire other people to do something they otherwise would not have the courage to do.

One morning that February, after the final guests left at 2 AM, I finally went to bed (my loveseat) only to wake up two hours later. I couldn't go back to sleep for the life of me, so I got up. There was still warm coffee in the large coffee urn, so I drew a cup and put on my cozy sweater.

I remembered the book idea, so I sat down at the computer, intending to make an outline of chapters—things that had happened at The Open Door Cafe. By the time the girls got up and started getting ready for church, not only had I constructed the outline, but the prologue practically wrote itself. Those words just kind of jumped out. Not only that, I knew the first sentence, I knew the last sentence, and I had typed up release forms for people to sign so that I could use their characterizations.

Yeah. It was a nice diversion, like a new hobby. For several months, I didn't even really think about it. It was just kinda on the back burner.

So then, months later, as I sat at the computer, the Voice came— for three nights in a row. I wouldn't even be thinking about writing. Sometimes, I was just playing Mah Jong (a type of Chinese card game played with tiles) on the computer. I was trying to best my record time of 2 minutes and 14 seconds matching a hundred-some-odd tiles. There I was, minding my own business, goofing around... and the "still small voice" would interrupt.

"You know, you really *could* be working on the book, instead of wasting time playing a game."

"*I said, I'm not going to work on any book until the Lord tells me to write one. I'm done with The Caron Show.*" I thought.

I know what you're thinking, but honestly, I'm just not that smart. Night after night, every time I would be sitting at the computer I would get the conscience message.

The next day was Friday. Payday. I went into the bank and filled out a deposit slip. When I gave it to the teller, she corrected a math error I made.

"As you can see, I majored in English for a very good reason— I'm math challenged." I quipped, laughing.

"Oh. So did I" replied the teller. "Are you a teacher?"

"No, I'm a writer." I blurted out without even thinking.

WHERE DID *THAT* COME FROM? It was just like the time Ellen asked me what I really wanted to do, and without a second thought I asserted that I wanted to run a coffee house from my home.

"Oh. What are you writing?"

I was in it now, but strangely the answer came tumbling out.

"I'm working on a project about how I ran a coffee house from my Victorian home, despite the fact I'm a single mom. There were lots of people who came to it and a lot of them got married— to each other."

"What an interesting story! I can't wait to read it. I write science fiction."

I thanked her, surprised by how encouraged I felt, and turned to go.

"Ma'am?" She called after me.

I turned around with my hand still on the doorknob.

"You forgot your money..."

As I walked across the brick walkway to my car, I apologized to God — again. "God, this is stranger than science fiction. Lord, I'm sorry. I'm doing it again—jumping the gun. I'm sick of me. I won't work on a book— or anything *else* for that matter, until *You* give me the go ahead."

Days passed without incident. Then, on Tuesday, I went to my church's prayer group, which they held in the multipurpose room. Some days the chairs were still up, and other days they were put away for UpWard Basketball. That night they were put away.

Now, I'm the sort of person who has to walk around when I pray or I get sleepy and my mind wanders. I admit it. If I have to sit during a prayer meeting, I'll be the one with my head leaning in my hands, struggling to keep from slumping in my chair. Maybe you do the same thing. Anyway, I found that if I walked around, it kept me more focused and alert. So, I was praying as I walked—for the youth group and the parents, for the little kids and the pastor.

One of the ladies was standing near me. After a time, she came up to me and spoke in hushed tones so she wouldn't distract the others.

"Caron, you've been on my mind all day. I think God wants me to tell you something."

"Okay—." Now, I wasn't *really* skeptical, I just wasn't sure what God would want to say to *me*. Okay, maybe that is skepticism.

"I just feel He wants me to tell you to not be discouraged because the little shop didn't work out behind The Golden Lamb. *It's only a small part of something much, much bigger.*"

I had heard this before... a *couple of times* before. Here it comes...

"And..."she continued, hesitating. "He wants you to go ahead with— a book."

At this point, I didn't know if I should laugh or cry. I think I was doing a little of both.

"He's going to bring to your mind all *kinds* of things that happened at your coffee house— and you're supposed to put them in the book... It will bless people all over the country because it will tell them how you did it."

She didn't know the *half* of it.

"I know, Barb." I whined. "It's called *Saturday Night at the Open Door Cafe*. I know what the first sentence is, and I know what the last sentence is. The prologue and the first chapter are written and so are the release forms."

At that point, she got tears in her eyes and was laughing.

"I thought you would think I was nuts!" she whispered.

"No, but I'm not really sure about me, though!" I said. "This has been going on all week." I then explained to her about the voice of my conscience I was getting when I was wasting time on the computer late at night.

So at that point, I set about the writing of what you have been reading.

During the next few weeks, people kept calling me about the cafe. I told them I wasn't hosting it any longer, that I was seeking some direction about what I was to do next, yadah, yadah, yadah... I was faking my way through it. There were times that I wasn't sure what to tell them. Maybe I should have just leveled with them, as in:

"Well, you see, I jumped the gun and rented a place, promptly was downsized where I worked for the *third* time in *four* years, and now I'm licking my wounds in the desert— thank you very much."

When I would pray and ask God about whether I should start up the cafe again, I would immediately think of when Jesus told Peter to "Feed my sheep." My mind would always return to that verse. What did He mean? Did He want me to open the cafe back up? Is *that* what He meant, meet people's need?

One night, I think it was in late August or early September, a woman named Mary called and shared her story. She needed a place to find support and encouragement as she was going through the final stages of a divorce. She had tried unsuccessfully to reconcile a marriage that she had not chosen to leave. I told her I wasn't hosting the cafe any longer, but that we could still meet for coffee. (I felt like a rat.) We agreed to meet at the Village Ice Cream Shop. The only problem was, I forgot to ask her how I would recognize her.

A few minutes before seven I came in through the rear entrance from the parking lot and sat down at one of the tables. I came a few minutes early so that I could see if a single lady came in—and I told the waitress that I was supposed to meet someone there, but forgot to ask what the lady looked like. There were some groups of ladies in the shop at three different tables and a woman sitting alone at a small round table by the wall, and a group of men in the back. I glanced at the woman sitting alone, wondering if it was Mary, but didn't want her to think I was staring at her. I looked at the clock— it wasn't quite seven yet. Surely Mary wouldn't come there *early*, even though that is exactly what I had done. The waitress came by and asked me if I wanted to order coffee while I waited, so I agreed. She walked away and the woman sitting by herself glanced at me. I smiled and then frowned a little, laughing, and mouthed the word, "Mary?"

She smiled back and mouthed, "Caron?"

We both laughed out loud and I got up and moved over to her table. We spent the evening talking about her marriage and she shared with me the incredibly difficult time she was having understanding why things had gone so wrong when she had tried so hard to have a Christian marriage. I had heard these things before.

Then we talked about the cafe and she urged me to give it another try. If so many good things had happened there, who was to say that the trend wouldn't continue? God must have something up His sleeve, I said.

All I knew is that they were Really Big Sleeves.

It was getting late and the ice cream shop was closing for the evening. She had parked her car in the back too, quite near my own car. She asked if she could stop by for a moment to see my house. I warned her that there was still a lot of furniture in the middle of the rooms that I hadn't maneuvered into place yet.

She came in and I led her around the 'Furniture Store' decor. She didn't seem to mind the early chaos decor and in fact, made me feel quite normal... Then we sat and prayed that God would make a way to reopen the coffee house and Mary left. I had a lot of soul searching to do.

Was God finished, or was *I*?

The fact was, people were still in need of what the cafe provided for them. That week there were three more calls from people about the cafe. Mary called faithfully too, every few days and volunteered her help.

October was coming on and I recalled the first meetings of The Open Door Cafe. What better time to open your doors than autumn, when the night air chills you to the bone and your breath hangs in the air with the smell of wood burning in someone else's fireplace (one of my cheap thrills)? What else *could* I do? Aw, what the heck...

I wallpapered the study and bought some more mugs.

The first week in October I re-opened my door to scores of single Christians, some of them the familiar faces I'd grown to love, and every one of them was dear to me. There was Jeff (known as "Jeff Z" to the early morning listeners of his radio show) who always wore Hawaiian shirts and reminded me of Wolf Man Jack. He was a wealth of information about old movies and television series— especially the music scores. There was Cotton Amburgy, who always embraced the learning of something new and was eager to share it along with his opinion. John— who would soon meet Jodi and change both of their lives forever. Mark and Vickie, Gary, all the folks from Connersville, and Steve— they all came back and we met weekly along with many others— for another year and a half!

Mary, after many months of helping me in every way with the cafe, eventually met her husband to be (also named Mark) who, up to that point was a forty-year-old *confirmed* bachelor. Not only that, but Mary's *daughter* consequently met *her* husband— through Mary's Mark, and a friend who came with Mark the first night met her husband to be. That was a three-for-one.

In all, there were *twenty people* who met their mate at my home and there are others I recently found out have become engaged. Others met treasured friends there and I hear they still get together regularly to attend plays and movies.

My oldest daughter, Maureen had gone to Haiti on a mission trip and then spent a year in the ministry in Atlanta; she then came home and met her husband to be. They too, came to the cafe on Saturday nights to hang out with those who Maureen originally called "the Old People" three years before. My youngest daughter, Emmy, who had always helped so much to prepare desserts for the cafe, became a good cook and loves to try out recipes to this day.

I learned later on that a woman who had only come once, loved the cafe and went back to her own church and started the same thing there. I had no idea what would be the long term results of the Open Door Cafe, but from time to time I learn that someone's life has changed forever because of what happened there.

I had lived in my home for four and a half years. For almost four of those years it was in foreclosure. A friend who worked in the mortgage industry most of his life, said incredulously when I explained things to him, "Caron, things like this just don't happen in this business." Then he added *"I think God hid you in the paperwork."* I had lived waiting for the other shoe to drop for all those years that I ran the cafe.

The house, beloved and so earnestly sought for, had become a burden too great to bear.

Chapter 18

One evening in early May I held the last meeting of The Open Door Cafe.

There was an unusually small turnout, and it was a rather somber evening. As it turned out, some of the regulars thought I said the *following* Saturday would be the final meeting of the cafe, and were quite sad to find that it was all over before they had had a chance to properly bid farewell.

Toward the end of the evening, Mark and Vickie came. I was so excited to see them, because it seemed fitting that since they were the first of the couples who met and married from the Open Door Cafe, that they should be there on the final night. They had been hanging posters for an upcoming concert nearby and Mark said he felt "they should come and visit". They had no idea that it was the final meeting.

Vickie was talking with some friends in the dining room—one of her friends from Connersville who had come by herself— and Mark came into the living room to talk. Jeff had been talking to me and decided to make some tea.

Mark sat across from me in one of the white wing chairs he had flopped in three and a half years before, and I was sitting on the taupe empire loveseat. Candles in a silver tray on the coffee table flickered feebly, and seemed to match the winding down of the mood. But Mark was energized.

"I felt I should share something with you— when I was driving over here. I didn't know this was your last meeting of the coffeehouse, but *now* I know that's why I'm supposed to tell you this." He folded his hands and looked at me. I was ready.

"Do you know anything about eagles?"

Huh? That was definitely not what I was expecting.

"Well, a little. My pastor spoke about them one time." I was waiting to compare notes between Mark and my pastor. I also wondered where he was going with this.

"Well, then, you know that an eagle is a real bad bird." He drawled. "It doesn't have any predators. Except condors. But the eagle was created with an advantage. If it's being pursued by a condor, it will fly toward the sun because it has a special eyelid that a condor doesn't have. Eagles can fly really high, too. Windshield's of jet planes have been busted out by salmon which were dropped by eagles flying *higher than the jet.*

"The point is, nothin's gonna mess with an eagle." He looked at me matter-of-factly, and continued.

"Anyway, at a certain point in it's life, the eagle gets pretty sorry. It gets all ugly and it loses its feathers. Its beak gets all crusty and it doesn't eat." He paused and looked at me, then added, "It's just a mess."

It was almost comical, but I listened because it was one of those Moments of Truth.

"Eventually he gets so ugly and his beak is so crusty that he can't hunt for food any more. His mate has to bring him food. If he takes the food, his mate will have to feed him for the rest of his life. They mate for life, by the way. He essentially stops being the eagle. He stops being what he was created to be. They usually don't live very much longer after that." He paused. *"Oo-r-rr"*

"And...?" I prodded. I wasn't sure I liked this story, especially the part about being a mess and pretty sorry— or, well, worse.

"Well, if he *doesn't* take the food, then one day, for some unknown reason, he starts banging his beak on a rock until all the crusty material comes off. Then he takes off flyin'— and he soars up ... *wa—aa-y* up." He gestured with his hand in a soaring motion. "And you know what? He never looks back. The amazing thing is, he's actually *better and flies higher than ever before.* He has to prove he's back.

It was quiet for a moment.

"God told me you're like that eagle, Caron. I don't know what you plan to do next, since you aren't doing your coffee house any more, but—— while I was driving over here tonight it was as clear as could be that I'm supposed to tell you this.

"You're gonna go through a time when you're all uglied out. You're gonna lose your feathers— and you're gonna be grounded. But during that time, God's gonna be working in you. And when He's done, you're gonna take off flyin' and you're gonna go higher than you've ever gone before."

"*Really?*" I was hopeful. But I wasn't looking forward to the uglied-out part. Or being grounded. In fact, I really wasn't sure I liked this story at all.

"You're going to fly higher, accomplish more, and it's going to bless a whole lot more people."

"Well, Mark, heck, it's *always* been about other people."

Vickie came through the French doors into the living room.

"Hey, did she tell you that tonight's the last night of the coffee house?"

"Yes, that's what Valerie was just saying. What are you going to do next?"

I was thinking, '*I'm going to be an ugly bird that can't fly*" —— but I told her that I didn't have any immediate plans.

Soon, Mark and Vickie, along with the others who came that night left amidst hugs and well wishes. Cotton was the last to leave— he said he felt he should stay with me a while.

I closed the door and watched through the lace curtain as Cotton walked to his car and drove away. I turned off the porch light and turned around to look from the front door in the foyer in through the French doors to my left at the lovely red walls and then into the dining room where so many of us sat late at night and shared Life. I walked through the rooms, blowing out candles, taking a cup and saucer to the kitchen, straightening a chair.

Then I sat in the study where the candles flickered in the fireplace. It had once been my bedroom and still was, though for three and half years I slept on the loveseat there. I thought of all the people who had gathered there, all their faces flashed to mind. I could almost hear their voices.

I got up and went over to the fireplace. I lifted the screen and set it aside, and one by one blew out the candles. I would never do this again, I thought to myself. The candle wicks were only fading embers, and smoke curled thinly upward then vanished.

I realized I had a camera with film in it, so I took pictures of all the rooms.

Once more sitting on the loveseat that had been my little bed for so long, I remembered back to when I was in the third grade. My family had lived in an old house, but we were going to move to what was called a "sub-division." It was a new invention.

The last day at my old school, which was moving day, I had hoped that the class would say goodbye. I even lingered after school, hoping that my teacher would say goodbye or maybe even tell me that she had enjoyed having me in her class. But after cleaning out my desk and gathering my papers and construction paper projects in my arms, I left the room, saying goodbye to my teacher. I don't think she heard me because she didn't turn around.

I walked home—it was a mile and a tenth—just as I had walked every day for three years (they didn't offer kindergarten at that school at the time). It had snowed, being February, and some of the sidewalks weren't shoveled. Some of the streets didn't actually have a sidewalk at all. I wanted to walk as slowly as I could, since I knew that I would never do it again. I had walked that way so many times before.

I remembered the time my mom walked over to the school with my little brother, Patrick, who was two and half to make sure that my sister, Colleen, and I didn't dawdle on the way home. There were tornado warnings that day, and as we hurried home the sky was dark navy blue and leaves and papers were swirling around through the air. We reached our front porch just as it started to rain and then hail. There wasn't a tornado after all, but from then on we knew to hurry home when it looked ominous outside.

I thought of all three first-days-of-school through grades one through three; of walking past the scary house, a brick Italianate home with its rounded windows and a huge pine tree in the yard. Of hurried trips past the gigantic sycamore tree with it's dappled gray and white bark and whose limbs, bent and gnarled, reached downward with creepy arms that just might scoop up an unsuspecting child walking home from school. I remembered the small blue house with the enormous icicles that hung from the roof's edge and its cheerful tinkling glass wind chimes that were not so common in those days as they are now.

On I walked, slowing myself if I forgot and started to walk too fast. I would see over the pile of papers in my arms the toes of my red snow boots alternately appear and disappear beneath the hem of my tweed coat. Right-left, right-left. Into puddles, into snow, back on the sidewalk, onto the street where the sidewalk stopped in oblivion and back onto the sidewalk again. A paper slipped from my arms and fell into a puddle, iridescent on top, with oil from the asphalt. I leant down and gingerly picked it up, soaking my mitten, and too late to keep the watercolors from smearing. On I walked, aware that the birds were singing despite the wintry scene, for spring was to follow, not too far behind.

When I neared my house, I thought that I must try to sit once more on the swings in the back yard, where we had been trapeze artists in the circus, where my sister and I had made houses in a pair of grotesquely shaped trees; and where we had baked mud pies on the metal swings in the sun.

I realized that if I went into the house, my mother would make me stay inside. I knew that she wouldn't understand *why* I wanted to sit once more on the swings and think back to summer days. She didn't understand at all how I thought about things. I was the quiet one in our family. Maybe I was just shy. Often, the interior world of the artist, the writer, or the composer is a mystery to others. So instead of walking up the front walk, I walked up our neighbor's driveway and went into the back yard.

I had a little trouble getting on the swing since I was always really small and my hands were full of papers, but managed to inch my way onto it. From my precarious perch, I surveyed the winter scene all around me, with the snow clinging and then falling from the bare trees. I thought back to summertime; of climbing those trees and pretending I could fly with my newspaper-and-tree-branch-Peter-Pan-wings and a wild leap into thin air, only to land with a realistic thud in the grass. Once, I leaped and landed on my bike, which leant all new relevance to the term, "Look before you leap." I was suddenly startled by my mother calling out the back door.

"What on *EARTH* are you doing on the SWINGS in the SNOW? Don't you know its *WINTER*?!"

Winter? I just *knew* there had to be a reason for all that snow. I knew she wouldn't understand. I was eight years old, but I had *that* figured out.

"Hurry up and wash your hands for dinner. You're all going to spend the weekend at your aunt's house."

I was grateful she sent me upstairs. I wanted to see my bedroom one last time. I climbed the stairs in the early twilight and went into my bedroom. The voices downstairs seemed to fade away as I entered the room I had shared with my older sister. I crossed the bare wood floor that was so cold in winter that when you got out of your warm bed you skittered across it in your bare feet to the warmth of the hallway rug.

I stood where my bed had been. It was disassembled, as was my sister's, and it leaned up against the wall. Being eight, I decided I should lay down on the floor as if I was once more in my bed, and look at the two windows with the door in the middle that opened out onto an upper story porch. Many were the summer evenings when I listened to other kids playing outside because it was "our bedtime".

Jeepers, it wasn't even dark out.

I laid down on the cold hardwood floor in my dress and leotards, trying my best to engrave the scene on my memory. Trying to pretend it was my bed once more. The fading bluish light of dusk coming in the windows, the streetlamp that flickered and then came on, the closet where the monsters and the scary big Patty Dolls were (I was sure they had sharp teeth), the light from the bathroom that fell upon the wall. I stared long and wide-eyed at the windows of my room, burning the vision into my memory.

For weeks, since we found out we were moving, I had looked forward to it. But it all came too fast and now it was time to go. I wasn't ready and there was no turning back.

I had said goodbye, in my own way, to a part of my childhood. When Monday morning came, I would be at a new school, meeting new kids, living in a new house that no one else had ever lived in. A new house, where no Christmas had been, no catching of fireflies in a jar in summer, no tears and no laughter. John Kennedy was still our President and would be for two more years. There were segments on the NBC evening news with Chet Huntley and David Brinkley about a man named Martin Luther King, and I saw white policemen beating people of color in a place called Alabama. And I had no idea there was a country named Vietnam.

But I *had* to remember the way it *was*, there in the old house, the home of my childhood, because *even then* , as a little girl, I was keenly aware of the terrifying beauty of the gift of days we have here on earth.

When I awoke, I was sitting almost exactly as I had been sitting when I fell asleep on my loveseat. The cafe was over and I was to embark on a new adventure—— that of being an ugly flightless bird.

Chapter 19

The days ahead would be busy ones. I needed to pack. In three weeks we would be moving into a new duplex, that, though it was on the other side of town, it was still less than 10 minutes away. I had signed a lease on it just two weeks prior. We had been living in the shadow of an unknown fate and had struggled against so many obstacles for so long that it felt as if my children and I were holding up the house. We all felt as if it was weighing us down.

"Just be careful, kids. We aren't out of the woods yet, just because we're moving doesn't mean that we're in the clear."

I don't even know why I said that. We had been so used to persevering in adversity, so accustomed to our gallows humor in the face of peril, that we felt we could handle most anything that came along. Sometimes, though, it felt like Adversity loomed, large and ominous, just over our shoulder, nipping at our heels as we tried to outrun it.

Several days passed and I found myself saying it again. Then I added, "You know, make sure you're wearing your seat belts— like when you go out with your friends."

A day or two passed. The previous Saturday, the final night of The Open Door Cafe, I was lighting the candles in the fireplace. I was thinking of what I had told the girls. *"Why had I said that?"* I wondered. There wasn't any *logical* reason to say it, only a vague sense of caution. I decided I was glad I had cautioned them, though, and stood up. In a split second, I blinked— and I was seeing in my thoughts a side view of my white Subaru. It startled me and I immediately thought, "So...it won't be in someone *else's* car, but *my* car." Why would I think that? It made no sense to me and I dismissed it as undisciplined wanderings of my thoughts— an overactive imagination.

Monday morning, as I dropped Abbie and Emmie off at school and Cricket at work and made my way to the intersection where I turned north to go to toward Xenia, where I worked at the international headquarters of Athletes in Action, a sports ministry. I put on my seatbelt. I have always been terrible about remembering to put it on. But, as I was sitting at the traffic light, I slipped it into place and hearing the click, thought I mustn't give the adversary of our souls any opportunity to mess with my family.

Thursday was an ordinary day. Running late, I had to stop and get gasoline before I dropped everyone off. I didn't have time to stand there at the gas pump, so I only put three dollars worth in because that was what was in my blazer pocket. I set off to deliver kids to their various places of work and school before the drive northward,

The drive was picturesque. I reached Waynesville, a small antique-y town 7 miles north of Lebanon, and had to stop for the red light. I felt antsy. I wanted to listen to music, but I had taken my tapes I usually listened to inside the night before. I didn't want to fiddle around with the radio because the reception wasn't very good. I needed some encouragement and sometimes I had a tape in the car from church services I had found particularly inspiring. Looking briefly in the glove box, I didn't see anything at first. But I found one on the bottom, underneath the manual and put it in the cassette player.

It was from a church service— about four years before. As it played, I gradually recognized the sermon. It was the Biblical story of Joseph, the youngest son of Jacob. His life was a story of overcoming in the aftermath of adversity. Time after time, though sometimes obscured by dire circumstances, most of which were unfair, Joseph overcame great obstacles to achieve his calling. His destiny.

I realized why I had gotten a copy of the sermon, for it paralleled my own life. It was not just about overcoming in adversity, but of realizing your potential, your gifts and calling. Sometimes the detours are long and full of peril. There are times when people will betray you, people who, to the trusting soul, say all the right things, but they have another agenda. There are times when you wonder if God really is in the thick of it with you. Sometimes, you question your sanity— as if you have some Messiah Complex. Would that we *all* did.

I settled into the drive northward along one of Ohio's scenic byways. The tape was full of advice. To stay the course, to refuse compromise, to hold fast to the vision of your life, to do everything with integrity, to realize that though it may take a long time— sometimes a lifetime— God is faithful and will bring about your destiny.

Before I knew it, the drive was over and I was winding my way slowly up the long driveway that led to the office where I worked. All day, the tape proved to inspire me. I realized that the life of Joseph could parallel anyone's life—and that no matter what situations we faced in life that we could be certain that there was a point to all of it. Joseph's life illustrated that one thing was always predicated upon something else, and that *each step in the process was necessary to set the stage for the step to follow.* Every situation in life is predicated upon a situation or need before it, and it is all woven together to form a grand tale. Even in the worst of situations there can be good that comes of it, even if, at the time, the outcome remains a mystery.

Later that day I left to take the mail to the post office in a white plastic tub. There was usually a lot of mail, as some of the staff members sent hundreds of letters to supporters. I put my seatbelt on and drove over to the post office. The tape was running from where I had turned the car off in the morning. It was at the end of the service. I thought as I turned the corner to enter the parking lot "Oh yes, I remember this part exactly."

I got out and carried the tub over to the back dock and joked around with one of the postal employees. They recognized me because I was there a lot and we always had a friendly-fire banter. I got back in and rounded the corner to the exit. Another carrier was standing at the exit and I motioned for them to cross. He smiled and gestured for me to cross, to which I started laughing and said out my window,

"Hey, *you're* the pedestrian!" So they crossed the exit and I pulled out onto the street. The traffic was backed up so I had to wait to get onto the main street. I was listening to the tape as I waited.

"Some of you know you have a calling", said the pastor on the tape. "—a dream that you know God has placed in your life. Maybe it's been such a long time in coming to fruition that you've even given up hope that God could bring it to pass. I'd like to ask you to step forward so that we can pray with you."

I reached forward to stop the tape. I remembered vividly walking forward during that service. I had tears in my eyes, there in my car. And I prayed all over again the very same prayer they prayed for everyone that day.

"Lord, don't let me miss it, whatever You do! I want to fulfill the things I've been told to do, the things You've promised to do through me. Whatever those "Big Things" are. I just don't want to be looking in one direction and miss what You have for me in another direction. You know how I am— I seem to do things by accident. Lord, sometimes I feel like heaven's Village Idiot!"

I looked down at the passenger's seat. I was reading *The Power of a Praying Wife*, by Stormie Omartian, and the book was lying there. I wasn't a wife, but someday hoped to be one. I was praying for my husband — not that I would get one, but I figured I would pray for him *before* I knew him, as I have often done. I pray that he is safe and committed to his own growth, that he becomes all he was meant to be, that he increases in kindness, in love, in integrity

I realized that a pedestrian on the corner was staring at me talking to myself in my car. *"He must think I'm crazed."* I thought. The light changed and I was relieved to be able to drive off.

"Lord, You know I would step forward all over again." I said "Just don't let me mess up. Don't let me miss it."

Exactly eleven minutes later, God would answer my prayer at a distant intersection, at combined speeds of 75 miles per hour.

Chapter 20

Perhaps he was just confused.

He was in the oncoming left turn lane of a four lane highway, and he leaned forward impatiently with his arms draped over his steering wheel, glancing from side to side— at the cross traffic. I saw him from a distance in a large vehicle with an expansive windshield as I rounded the gradual bend in the road. The sun was shining in the windshield and I flipped down the visor. It was then that I saw him put his turn signal on, *still looking at the cross traffic.*

"What's he doing?!" I exclaimed aloud.

My light was green and I was going the speed limit as I approached the intersection. There was another vehicle, a white work van with ladders, headed the same direction as I in the southbound lane, preparing to turn left—between the other driver and myself.

"He's going to turn—he's looking at the cross traffic!" I thought. He wasn't looking at the *oncoming* traffic, and even if he did, at that time the white work van—the same color as my car— was preventing him from seeing me. *"He can't see me!"*

I instinctively started to apply the brakes but suddenly realized that I had forgotten to put my seatbelt back on when I left the Post Office parking lot. If I tried to stop, I would skid into him and go through the windshield. Calculating my speed and the distance in an instant, I realized that my only chance to survive an impact was to try to get through the intersection as quickly as possible. The best accident would be the one I didn't have. My foot was above the brake pedal but instantly, without my even thinking about it depressed the gas pedal. I accelerated into the intersection, bracing myself and steered slightly wider to the right to give myself some added inches, then corrected so I wouldn't hit the guard rail..

Time strangely slowed way down.

I thought he would miss me, but then there was a terrible grinding sound of metal and a powerful abrupt shove sideways. I braced myself, my eyes shut, gripping the steering wheel, holding as tightly as I could. Everything went dark then light, then dark and light again. The centrifugal force made it almost impossible to hold on any longer and I feared I would let go. But incredibly, I had the strangest feeling of being in the exact center of the spinning of the car, like an LP on a turntable with a fixed center, *and the rest of the accident was going on around me.* It was the weirdest feeling. Just when I thought I could hold on no longer, the back end of my car violently hit the guard rail and came to a stop. Everything was still for a moment and then I felt both rear tires, brand new only two months before, simultaneously deflate.

My car was still running (which I thought a little amusing) and the traffic was stopped, so I pulled my car over, wobbling on the wheel rims, behind his and tried to open the door.

The driver came running over to my car. "You alright?" he asked. Then added, "You're not gonna open *that* door."

All I could think was, *not now.* I have too much to do. Why did this have to happen now?

"I don't know what in the world I was thinkin'" he commented, looking at the intersection. He must have realized that in his hurry and impatience he was looking in the wrong direction, instead of the oncoming traffic which had the right of way.

There was broken glass in my hair, down inside my clothes, on the dashboard and the seats from the window directly behind me on the driver's side. I could hear approaching sirens, of fire trucks. Momentarily a police officer opened the passenger side door and told me to stay where I was, but I felt desperate to get out of the car, if only to prove to myself that I could, so when he stood up to go talk to another officer, I climbed out over the gear shift and stood on solid ground.

The ground was solid— only my *knees* were like jelly.

Two paramedics came over to me and started asking me questions, then asked me to sit down inside the ambulance. As I talked with them inside, the police officer came over and stood at the door.

"Ma'am, are you sure you had your seat belt on?"

"Yes, I remember putting it on when I left work for the Post Office."

Puzzled, he shook his head and walked away toward the vehicle that hit my car. A moment later, he walked back to my car dragging white parts of my car along with him. The paramedics were asking me if my blood pressure was always that high.

"No, it's usually pretty low."

"We'll wait a minute and take it again. So, where do you work?"

"Athletes in Action—I used to run a coffee house too."

"Oh, yeah. I've heard a lot about Athletes in Action. Sports Ministry, right? So, who's the president —of the United States?"

"I thought you meant of Athletes in Action.... George Bush—the second one.

A coffee house— where?"

"Well, I ran it from my house..."

"A house? Oh, I thought it was a shop. That's unusual, why your house?"

"It's kind of a long story, so I'm writing a book about it." I told them a little bit about it and about my old house. The man who was taking notes and asked me questions told me he and his wife owned an old house a few blocks away, there in Waynesville. We talked about old houses and he took my blood pressure again which was considerably lower.

I could see out the rear window of the ambulance that a big group of firefighters and police officers were standing around my car. Must've been a guy thing.

The police officer was at the door again. "Ma'am, are you *certain* you had your seat belt on?"

"Well, I remember putting it on right before I left the parking lot of AIA." I had completely forgotten I even went to the Post Office.

He smiled slightly. "You know, I found your outer door. It was wedged up under this guy's grill. And your rear bumper? It was attached to his car too. Do you know you did a couple of 360's?' he grinned. "Are you hurt?"

"I don't think so— I'm not really sure."

He suddenly directed his attention to the paramedics. "Hey, make her lay down there— and put that neck brace on."

"You heard the man."

So I laid down on a hard board and they fitted me up with something that seemed like it was wrenching my neck There was broken glass chunks down my back, in my pockets of my blazer, in my shoes.

"You're a pretty lucky lady, you know that?" The officer asserted and walked away again, shaking his head.

It's amazing the luck you have when you pray real hard.

Later that night, Maureen and her fiancé came and picked me up at the urgent care facility. While I waited for them, I thought of what Mark had told me about the eagle only six days before. Was this the grounded part? I had no car, and I was sure that the insurance company would try to get out of giving me what my car was worth. I was already stiff, and I had to move to a new residence in three weeks.

When I got home, the girls were at the dining room table. One of them joked, "Hey, mom, what's for dinner?"

I tried to act as if everything was okay, and went in to get something out for dinner. I talked to the girls from the kitchen, and they were looking at each other.

"Mom, what did you say?"

"You keep saying dumb stuff."

"I'm a little weirded-out, I think." I realized I was struggling to talk. I knew I had hit my head, but they didn't seem to be concerned about it at the urgent care, so I didn't know that I should be. I felt like I had just woken up and hadn't had my morning coffee. So I made a pot of coffee and tried to remember if I had all the ingredients for beef stroganoff.

"I'll make dinner, mom. " said Cricket (we always called her that). "Why don't you go sit down or something?"

So the girls made dinner and I went in and sat on my bed/loveseat. What was this all about, anyway? I had been so glad, only a few days before, that I was healthy and that I had a reliable car, that I had a nice job and we would be moving to a more stable situation. Now, my car was gone, I was not in the best of shape and we had to move in three weeks.

The next day, I did not go to work When I came on board only two months before, the organization had, itself, only occupied the building it was in a mere six weeks, so I came in when a lot of things were still in boxes. There was no process, no system of doing anything. It was a clean slate. I had worked to develop office procedures so it would run itself, and now I was about to find out if that was the case. I always found myself setting up processes or systems that you didn't have to baby-sit, but instead freed you to do more creative things.

I went outside and sat on the deck in the early May sunshine. I felt vaguely out of touch— disconnected with my surroundings. It was as if I was only an observer watching myself carry on my actions without really feeling, seeing, hearing. It was the weirdest feeling. The sun seemed too bright, and reading made me feel a little dizzy. So I went inside and tried to write in my journal, which always made me feel centered and fixed, as if I could survey, from some higher plane, the terrain of my life and get my bearings. But I didn't feel like writing either, so I tried to sleep. I really felt exhausted. The mid- morning was usually my most productive time of the day, but all I really wanted to do was sleep.

I found, however, that the sleep was intermittent at best and filled with reenacting dreams of the accident. It was then that the realization came that I was, just the day before, and but for a miracle, looking Death in the face. I suddenly became afraid. Afraid of what *almost* happened. If not for some divine intervention in the form of being able to calculate the factors of the accident—my speed, his decision to turn, the distance between us both—instantly in advance, and not, contrary to instinct, applying my brakes, I would be dead and my daughters suddenly alone. Indeed, I had had advance warning in the weeks before, and somehow knew what was coming. Seeing the other driver looking from side to side— I almost recognized it for what I'd been warned of.

"*So this is it—this is the thing I was forewarned about*" I had thought in a half second. It was as if I could see a close-up of him, his expression and mannerisms, and it didn't make sense.. I've heard of how our subconscious recognizes things like license plate numbers at a crime scene, etc.

But in the waking of those fitful dreams, I realized I was *here.* I was here, on this good earth and that something tried to take me out. God had given me warning days before, and kept me safe in the midst of all of it. I had been spared.

But the question remained, *Why*?

Was it my prayer, tearfully and passionately repeated in my car— from a church service four years prior (and directly after I had passed the point where I would normally have put my seatbelt back on) that *saved* me? Was there a reason that I had taken all the music tapes out of my car the night before, and that I was at a red light when I needed to fish around in my glove box for a tape? If there hadn't been a red light, I wouldn't have bothered. Why was it the tape that it was —and *not* a tape on, say, walking in forgiveness, or being a good steward of our time, or a John C. Maxwell tape on leadership? Why was it a tape on destiny and purpose, and hanging on until your dream becomes reality? Why was it a tape that prompted me to pray so earnestly not fifteen minutes before an accident could quite possibly have ended my life?

I thought of the things I had left to do, the things that, if I were to stand before God, I would *wish* I had followed through on. Things that were, as yet, undone. And it came to me.

The book.

This book. *The one you are, at this moment, holding in your hands.* Something didn't want me to write it for you, and God *did.* There are roadmaps in these pages, maps to where you, yourself, are supposed to go, and encouragement for your journey—— and some of you are very excited reading this. You know the secrets these pages hold, and then again, *some* of you thought you were just a little crazy.

You didn't think it was really all about *me*, did you? Yeah, it's about a coffee house, but it's also about something *so much bigger.* It is all about destiny. *Your* destiny. And sometimes destiny hangs by a thread— or a prayer.

The next day I felt like I'd been hit by a train instead of a sport utility twice the size of my Subaru. If I had been driving any other car made the same model year, things would have been worse— much worse. Subaru met the 1997 side-intrusion protection standard (steel reinforcement bars inside the door panels) *years* before they were required by law to do so. Another "coincidence"?

I don't remember much of the day. I think I slept most of it. Cricket came in and asked me if I was okay. I told her that if I didn't feel better by that evening that I would go back to the hospital. Late that night I started to feel a little better.

But the next day, Sunday, was Mother's Day. I wanted to go to church, and struggled for the longest time to get dressed. My arms just didn't work right and I couldn't pull anything over my head or zip anything up in back because my shoulders hurt too much. I made myself go to church, if only to prove to myself that I could carry on. I needed the corporate worship of my fellow faithwalkers. In that service, I felt as if I was in the company of angels— I almost *was*, for that matter. I was so grateful to be alive.

Going to church was, however, very difficult and really exhausting.. I left when it was over and drove home in Maureen's old Buick. I probably shouldn't have been driving at all. The doors were so heavy that it was hard to open and close them. I came in through the front screen door that sunny Mother's Day, and into the dining room where the girls were scurrying around. One of them stepped aside, and there on the table were cheerfully wrapped presents. Positioned so that they emerged upward from a brightly colored gift bag, were gardening gloves holding flower seeds and a new trowel and cultivator. They were all standing around the table, proud as they could be with grins and smiles all around.

I stopped in my tracks and wept. To think, *I almost missed this!* I'm here, and these are my children, and it is Mother's Day. I almost wasn't *here*.

"Why are you sad, Mom? You're not supposed to *cry*." said Emmie. "It's all happy. See? Maureen put the gloves in there like they're holding the seeds."

I thought, "How can I explain to them how much it means to be here with them— when I almost *wasn't*?" To still be here on a beautiful spring day, or even an ugly rainy winter's day? To be here for my daughter's wedding, and the birth of my granddaughter that would come a year and a half later? The more I thought of how hard it was to explain, the more I cried. I was so very grateful to see the faces of my children— nothing in this world mattered more.

Of course, *they* didn't understand the full implications, they just thought their mom was nuts.

I didn't know it, but I had a concussion (as evidenced by my two black eyes when I reported to work two days later (it took someone in sports medicine to point it out— I just thought I felt really bad). For many weeks, things just didn't feel right. Everything felt just a little flat. Nothing was funny. The smallest things had a way of making me sad, and everything seemed overwhelming. I found it hard to organize anything to pack because I couldn't focus on anything. Where I was generally able to come into a situation and put it into order in the past, there seemed to be no way to make decisions, or think through anything.

We did eventually move, though much of it seems to be a blur. I think most of it was done by my daughters' male friends from school and work.

In the months ahead, I found it nearly impossible to go back over to the house. Not only did I not feel up to it, but the sadness I felt each time I was there was overwhelming.

In the course of department meetings at Athletes in Action, we had shared the short and remarkable stories of how we had gotten "from there to here", and one morning it was my turn (we had to go out of sequence because one of the members was sick). I wasn't at all prepared for what I would tell them. I shared not only the marvelous things that had happened in my life through unbridled risk taking, but also the not so pretty details. The strange thing is, *I had not intended to do so*, as I had meant to keep my private losses private.

Sharing my own story that day, however, opened me up to subsequent conversations over the coming months with my supervisor, Ron, and later with Toni.

We became good friends and very supportive of one another in our small, three-person department. Moreover, in sharing the wonderful things that had occurred in my life, I felt that the friends I had most recently made *must* understand the difficulty I was having moving beyond what I had lost. I struggled with it immensely, not understanding why everything that had been so very good had turned out so very bad.

I went back there to that house I had loved— and lost— in the darkness of night, in that dreadful December, with my friend and fellow adventurer, Ron.

And it was then that I remembered faintly, how once, so very long ago, I had feathers ——and *I could fly*.

Chapter 21

One should never say, "Never again." I thought I didn't want to host a coffee house ever again.

One week in November (before Ron and I had visited the old house on Main Street a few weeks later) as was our custom, Ron, Toni and I had our department meeting. We were discussing where we saw ourselves in the next five years.

"I don't know about you two, but I just feel like God wired me to sell coffee and dessert to people. I don't know when, where or how, but it's going to be an old building, see, and there's a porch on the side and .."

I ripped out a sheet of paper from my spiral notebook where I'd been taking notes for the meeting. "...And, see, there are going to be all these cute little windows all along the side where I'll have tables with little lamps on them right there at the windows. Maybe it's a farmhouse or something. And there'll be gaslights and— let's see, maybe park benches where people can eat their little pastries —oh, and a deck on the back for live Irish music"

For weeks, ever since the first turning of the leaves, I'd been thinking of how it would be to have a restaurant, a coffee house or bed and breakfast in an old farmhouse. I had this indescribable need to nurture and spoil people, to create a place where their need for comfort was so entirely met that they could focus on becoming whole, where there would be healing and restoration in their life. When I would drive down the many country roads that surround my small town, I would instinctively look at old houses.

"See, Lord. Something like that—— with all those cute little windows on the side." I would talk to God as if He was right next to me.

I held up the page for them to see. We were all laughing.

"We can all work together and it'll be fun, you'll see! We won't need meetings because we'll all be on the same page anyway, and we'll all know what needs to be done instinctively. We can have pumpkins and mums right by the door. In fact, maybe we'll sell pumpkins or something."

After our meeting, I crumpled the drawing up and threw it in the trash, and went back down to my office.

That same week, a woman at my church approached me and said, "Caron, there's someone you need to talk to— the lady who owns the coffee shop in town. She was telling me that since the weather turned colder she's had a lot fewer people in. I told her about your coffee house you used to do and how you missed it, and she'd like to talk to you."

Now, it's a really weird thing when you drive right past a place every morning and know you should go in and talk to the person, but your mind gives you every excuse on earth not to. And I didn't for four months, even though I drove past it taking the girls to school every morning.

One night, however, I went in with a friend to sit and talk over some coffee. I didn't know, despite the large, clearly worded signs, that we were to place our order at the counter. A woman approached the table and for some reason, I asked if she was the owner. She replied, "Yes."

"Oh... you know, I've been told I need to talk to you. I used to have a Christian Singles Coffeehouse."

"I know—I've heard all about it!"

We arranged to meet the following Monday.

When the time came to meet, I brought a copy of the article that appeared in the magazine, and a photograph of my old house. We talked for some time about what we saw as the role of her shop. She understood how I had been interested primarily in the ministry of the coffeehouse, not in the business aspect of it. She was most gracious, and since we were very similar in our artistic bent, we had the feeling of being sisters. Then she said the strangest thing.

"Well, you know, what I *really* need is help with our Sharonville store."

My first thought was, *"There's no way I'm driving down to Sharonville every week to do a singles function."* You see, there wasn't any quick and easy way to get to Sharonville from Lebanon without battling one-lane traffic with lots of left turns in front of you for mile upon mile. But I couldn't tell *her* that, so I said,

"Oh? What can you tell me about it?" I sipped the Milky Way latte she had made for me.

"Oh, you'd like it. It's in an old building....".

"Really?" I replied, mildly interested. I just didn't get it...

"Well, the City of Sharonville actually owns it. They remodeled it—it used to be an old house."

'*Really..*" the light was starting to flicker on.

"Yeah. There's the most wonderful *porch* on the side———"

I could hardly contain myself. Here it comes...

"———and *there are all these cute little windows— all along the side."*

I nearly dropped the latte in my lap!

"Wait! Is there a doorway where the windows are, where you could put pumpkins and mum—" I found it hard to sit still!

"I had mums there in the fall!"

"Is there a deck on the back, where you could have *music*?"

"Sure—and it's right there in the gaslight district!"

"Wait a minute..." the Doubting Thomas was rising up in me. "When you look at the front of the house, are the windows on the right or the left?"

Puzzled, she thought a moment. "That would be the right. Have you seen it?"

"'*Seen* it?' Kathy, I *drew* it! About four months ago— when Kelly first told me about you. The only thing is, I threw the drawing away."

The truth is, I'd been obsessed with the idea of a house/restaurant that looked the way she described it, and I even drew it—from a side angle and also from a top view— on a date. I think my date thought I was obsessed.

I probably was obsessed, which is good. I thought I was simply crazy.

It reminded me of another instance, many years ago, twenty four, to be exact, when my son was a toddler. He was playing with some toys on the floor, and I was in the kitchen doing dishes. I was looking at the dishes we had. They were, quite honestly the weirdest dishes I'd ever seen. They were given to us or we got them on sale or something. They were brown black and white with a weird design in the middle. But I had always loved blue and white dishes. I remembered when my mom got a set of Stafforshire Balmoral blue and white china. More recently, I had taken a liking to the pottery-type dishes popular at the time, with the iron specks and a blue rim around the edge. My sister had gotten some just like them for a wedding gift a couple of years before. As I dried them and put them in the cabinet, I prayed one of those off the cuff prayers:

"Lord, I know You have a lot of important things on Your mind, but one of these days, if You can see Your way clear, I'd really love to have some of those blue and white dishes with the rim—well, any blue and white dishes. If You wouldn't mind."

Can you believe I really prayed that? I sat the last cup in the cabinet and shut the door.

The next day after an evening service, I cam home and put my son to bed. Suddenly the phone rang and I hurried to answer it.

"Caron, this is Annette Hammel. Do you have a minute?"

"Sure."

"I don't know how to tell you this.... I think I'm supposed to give you some dishes."

"Really?"

My husband just gave them to me today, but for some weird reason, I think I'm supposed to give them to you. There's nothing wrong with them— they're still in the box."

"What color are they?" I was really thinking, *"Ah ha! I bet they're brown black and white."*

"Well, they're white."

I was thinking, *"Well, white's good. It will go with most anything."*

"Well, that's not quite right. They're white but they have a blue rim — *you know, with those little flecks in them.*"

What? I proceeded to relate how I had prayed only the day before for the dishes with the blue rim and flecks— which was the day that she had been given the dishes.

Did she know the impact her small act of obedience would have upon people reading about it here, *twenty-four years later*—as a total stranger reads these words at this moment? Is there a small act of obedience, whose origin is in someone's prayer, that has prodded you lately? What difference would it make, if you knew they would tell countless people many years later about something God used you to do?

Kathy and I made arrangements to go down to Sharonville the following week so I could take a look at the layout. All week long, Ron and I talked about the possibility of me leaving Athletes in Action — if the right opportunity came along.

The following Saturday there was a snow emergency declared and no one was permitted to go anywhere. Our appointment was rescheduled for the following week

The next Saturday, prior to our meeting, I was loading the dishwasher. I was anxious about the meeting. What was it all about? Did she want me to simply run a singles' function there once a week? I prayed silently, *"Lord, I don't know what you have in mind. Help me just to be a brave— I don't have to be chief. It's too bad she already hired a manager. Help me to learn how to use all the power tools, like that espresso machine, so that when I have my own place I'll know what I'm doing... But if you want, why don't You kinda get rid of that manager for me?"*

Okay. I know, I know. That was a terrible prayer, but I have to be honest, I really did pray that way. Not that I wanted God to *permanently* "get rid" of the manager. I just wanted to be able to afford to work there-- and there's not much of a profit margin in that business unless you're managing.

Also, I do, after all, hold the undisputed title of Heaven's Village Idiot.

Ten minutes later, we were driving along in her car. It was raining, but it sure beat the snow and ice we had the week before.

"Caron, had you thought of maybe working part-time in Sharonville?"

Part-time would just barely cover gas money in getting to Sharonville— I couldn't actually afford to work there.

"Well, Kathy, for the right opportunity, I'd work *full* time in Sharonville."

"What? You'd leave Athletes in Action? What about your benefits?"

"If the place looks anything like the drawing, I'll know I'm supposed to be there. I'll just have to believe that God will keep me well and safe."

"That's amazing. Things weren't working out with the current manager and we had to let him go... Bill and I were praying you would be willing to be the manager. Would you consider..."

"Would I con-*sid*-er? Yes!" I jokingly held my arm behind my back, as if she had to twist my arm or something.

After a few minutes of chatting and driving and chatting and *more* driving, we rounded the corner and the coffee shop came into view. It wasn't like what I had drawn four months before. It was *exactly* like what I had drawn.

We were both in tears by the time we walked inside. It was another Joseph story. There *had* to be a snowstorm the week before so that the manager would make a call to the city building to complain about the snow removal. I *had* to go into the coffee shop in Lebanon that first night so that I would meet the woman who owned it (*finally— after four months of putting it off*), and it was *all* timed around the snow — that had *not yet fallen*— and the drawing (now discarded in the trash) that had been done four months before.

When I got home, I just couldn't wait until Monday. I called Ron.

"Ron! You'll never guess what! She made me the manager of the coffee shop! I have my own *place*!"

Initially, there was silence on the other end. "Well good. That's really something." He was taking in the whole story and considering all the ramifications of what I was relating.

"And, Ron— it's *just like the drawing!*" I paused, no, actually I whined. "I just wish I hadn't thrown it away. I wonder if she really believes that there ever was a drawing at all!"

There was a short silence on the other end.

"Caron—" there was a long pause........... "I've got your drawing."

(Gasping on my end of the line). "What?"

" I took it out of the trash when you threw it away. I brought it home to show Jeri because I thought it looked like our old house. But I kept it. It's been in my wallet for four months. Something told me not to let you just throw it away."

Can you believe *that*?

I left Athletes in Action at the end of that week, exactly one year *to the day* after I came there. I felt that I had a clear unction from heaven, and this was borne out by the neat, tidy, immediate filling of my vacancy at AIA by another member who was, curiously enough, looking for an opportunity to assume more responsibilities.

I set about turning the coffee shop into a haven, a sanctuary for the tired soul. There were the white wing chairs, and even the antique mantle from my old house. I brought an antique Chinese screen, Victorian lamps, my hammered dulcimer, and oriental carpets. It looked like a home. People actually came in and took photographs of the interior.

Ron brought me the drawing, and I put it in a plastic sheet protector. I kept it in a notebook by the cash register along with a copy of the magazine article and a picture of my dear old pink house.

Why?

Because *countless* people came into the restaurant, from all walks of life and every circumstance; and for *some* reason, asked me:

"So...uh...how'd *you* get here?"

Now, stop a minute and think...when was the last time *you* went to the grocery store or the dry cleaners, or even to a cafe, and asked how the manager got there? It was *always* when it was down time— not a soul in the place. Often, though, they would say something stranger, like:

"You know, I don't even know *why* I'm here— " There was a nervous laugh, then: "I don't even *like* coffee." or,

"I was at work and something said, 'Go get coffee.' So I said to myself, 'Hey, we have coffee here at work'. And the voice says, 'No, *go* get coffee." So I'm drivin' along and I see this sign— and that's why I'm here." They would then pause and look at me.

That was my cue that it was a Divine Appointment— and in less than twenty seconds (sometimes I actually counted the seconds because I *knew* what would follow) they would proceed to tell me the reason *why* they were there. So I would wait for an answer I knew was to follow...

"I just found out I have diabetes."

"I miss my husband. We were married twenty-three years."

"I don't understand the change in my daughter. She's like a stranger."

"My cancer is back."

"I'm concerned for my neighbor's son—he's in Iraq."

I would answer that I had something important to tell them; that it was no accident or coincidence that they were there. "I'm going to tell you a remarkable story..." I would say as I reached for the black binder next to the cash register and opened it.

It was magic. I told them of the Open Door Cafe, of the pink Victorian I lost despite my best efforts, the twenty people who met their mate, my single mom-ness, the article in *Today's Christian Woman*, surviving a 75 mph collision with two major impacts, my daughters surviving a near fatal accident— *and how I drew the building where they now stood.*

Then, I would ask them if they wanted to step outside... for "a Field Trip".

No one— ever— said "No".

Suddenly, hope and anticipation would flicker across their faces. They knew I was going to show them something life-changing, and they were sorely in need of a miracle.

We went outside and onto the sidewalk.

I held up the black binder. They were anxiously awaiting the surprise.

"Are you ready?" I would ask.

"I've got Goosebumps." they would say; or,

"I've heard of things like this happening to *other* people, but..."

Slowly, watching their expression, I would raise the plastic page protector that covered the drawing, and there, detail for detail, right before their eyes, was the miraculous rendering of the reality.

Their eyes were full of wonder, and sometimes tears. They were incredulous and took the binder from me, looking from the drawing to the scene and back again. I would take the binder carefully and tell them that just as there was a plan for me, to bring me there to that place, that God had a plan— *their* plan—— and that He was just as surely leading them someplace full of wonder and promise. Their situation was under control, and just as I didn't have an answer for everything that had happened, I knew God was leading us, making a way. They were usually shaken and always grateful, and we often prayed together standing right there on that very sidewalk with traffic flying past us.

"Now," I would say. "go get *your* dream."

The interior of the shop was lovely, we had some great loyal customers, and the guest and comment book was *full* of compliments and gratitude.

Also, I worked about seventy-five hours a week— and that was only the hours we were open.

I was exhausted and my family missed having a mom. I was actually glad when I interviewed someone to work there to develop the corporate box lunch aspect— and she came back with a request to buy the restaurant! Kathy and Bill (who had overcome some major health issues that year) were actually ready to sell so that they would be free to pursue some other options.

The new owner didn't want me to stay because of the "too many cooks" thing, so I was essentially free to, well, *write what you are now reading.* This is the *verbal form of the drawing* I showed to so many people.

I've often wondered why I had to lose my house, why things just didn't work out right. I can only speculate that if I was still doing the Open Door Cafe, I would not have the opportunity to miss it so much; and in turn, I wouldn't have written about it so that you, yourself, could share that experience. It's the frustration of *not having* the cafe any longer, and not (at the present time) having the space to do it in that forms the fuel for writing this book; thereby creating the possibility that HUNDREDS of Open Door Cafe's could spring up all over the nation(s) —through the people, like yourself, that are reading it. For "some reason", *my* every attempt has been thwarted to re-open The Open Door Cafe.

Now think about it. How many people out there in huge churches are waiting for their church to offer a small group or cell group ministry to no avail? They've asked their pastor, they've asked again, they've even offered to coordinate it, to host it—and it falls on deaf ears. Instead, they are herded into church each Sunday to do their duty of sitting there and listening, but the pastor hardly knows their name. But what the flock really needs is an intimate setting where they can share their heart and struggles, and be given encouragement and support. They are in isolation hell.

What about the single adult? They are told they shouldn't go to bars to meet people, but where on earth are they going to meet someone? Sure, God *could* bring them a mate through their front door—after all, He is God, you know. But doesn't it make sense to have regular gatherings that are wholesome and enriching, where people are reasonably certain of being with other Christians, or at least people who aren't under the influence?

What about the college and career group, or the seniors in the community? Don't they long for the companionship of others in their shoes? Must they wait for the Quarterly Fellowship Pot Luck, and, on the spur of the moment, sit with a virtual stranger and be expected to share deeply? Or should there be an open forum night after services on an ongoing, weekly basis where people just meet and Get to Know Each Other?

After all, it isn't really all about *us*, is it?

What if the adversary of our souls doesn't *want* us to get together to compare notes and support one another? Isn't he all about division anyway? If Jesus' final prayer was for unity, then what in hell is going on? Wouldn't the enemy *want* us to be isolated in our faith, depending on the local Christian bookstore for vicarious fellowship?

For various reasons at the present time, every avenue for another Open Door Cafe is blocked for me. But I figure that if I can't have what I want, for whatever reason, I'll do everything within my power to make certain that others get *their* heart's desire. If my only means to have a cafe is to inspire *others* to do the same and create miracles in *their* life, then *this is my cafe*, in the words upon the page. And no accident, distraction, no financial trauma or auto accident can stop it.

Think of it this way. It's like when Jesus spoke of the seed that must die and fall to the ground before it can produce fruit. There's the appearance of loss (the "death" of the seed) but what results is something much greater. When you plant corn, you don't just get one corn. You get an *ear* of corn. You get a harvest. It multiplies exponentially.

Again, Jesus taught another parable— that of the wicked servant who buried his talent in the ground. The two other servants brought forth fruit, thirty, sixty and one hundred-fold from the talents they were given. Take the meaning of "talent" any way you want.

That's what this book is intended to do. This is *my* thirty, sixty and one hundred-fold. The cafe has the potential to become something much, much larger than it was in the beginning. *This is going to be big. It's going to be very big.* It took one small-redheaded-single-mom-person, who overcame a lot of awful things, to make a dream. Out of the ashes of great obstacles and terrible dark personal experience, came something that could transform lives. It gave hope to people who lost hope. It encouraged people to do something great. Out of loss came abundance. Out of shame, came triumph.

I bet you *never* look at the people sitting there in the church pews quite the same. Which of *them* is sitting on a dream, a talent, or a miracle?

What are *you* sitting on?

Oh. There's one more thing about never saying "never."

Chapter 22

I had to pick my daughter, Maureen, up from work after I left the coffee shop early one day, and I had to drive down Main Street where our old house was. It had been painted a lovely green with deep raspberry shutters by the new owners —— and there was a "For Sale" sign out in front!

"You should make an appointment to go through it, Mom." Maureen prodded. She was always full of mischief.

I shrugged and dismissed it —— to *her*. But after I got home I kept thinking about it. The next day, I mentioned it to Ron the next day.

"You know, if we went through it, you could see how it looks in the daylight." I suggested.

Maybe my apple, Maureen, didn't fall far from the tree.

He was agreeable, if only because it was another aspect of the mystery, another piece of the puzzle. Maybe there was a way that I *could* get it back. It always seemed to me that God was writing a grand story through me with all the events that had happened.

I called and the real estate agent answered my questions. The new owner was asking $45,000 more than I paid for it. I had tried to sell it for three years at *much less*. I'll never understand *that* one. I guess it was all in The Plan... or more accurately, the *mystery*.

At the appropriate time, Ron and I met at the house and the agent was running late. We stood looking at the house we had toured so long ago. How much had it changed? Would I even know the inside? Before long, an SUV sped up the street and turned, almost on two wheels, into the driveway. A woman with long hair got out and approached us, her hand extended. We made introductions around and then made our way toward the front door.

"They've changed *everything*." she said.

My heart sank.

Up two steps and onto the front porch, open the wooden screen door, fiddle with the latch, and there was still the "old house smell".

So far, so good.

Inside, the lights were on. A really bright chandelier was hanging in the front hall where there had been a ceiling fan. Okay, I was never really a fan of the fan. The floor was all light and bright from being refinished, where they had been dark from age. They were also extremely shiny from polyurethane. I had always liked the fact that the floorboards were so old and not necessarily pristine Their dark color seemed somewhat shabby in an elegant sort of way. Much like a house in the English countryside. They weren't, after all, supposed to look like the new floors in a sub-division house. The French doors were still there, and we made our way, at the leading of the agent, from room to room. The wallpaper had changed in every room.

"They just *gutted* the place." said the agent.

I wished she would just stop *saying* that! Had they really gutted it? We were not yet in the kitchen, and already I wanted to sit down and cry. Was it still charming, with the little wallpaper and the white cabinets? We moved from the living room to the study, once my bedroom.

"This is listed as a two bedroom, but you could use this room as a bedroom." she instructed.

I nodded in agreement. How well I knew...

We then entered the dining room. It seemed odd to me that the order of rooms we entered was the same as when Ron and I had toured the house all those months before. We turned to the left and entered the kitchen.

My kitchen.

The wallpaper was a bit larger in scale —well, *quite a bit* larger in scale, but the cabinets, the sink, the window above the sink, my little window— were all the *same*. I reached up and touched the dear little white glass-paned cabinets and then opened the small black latch of the window above the sink. The October air— that same sort of balmy, on-the-edge-of-autumn-gusting-now-and-then breeze— once again came through the screen, fragrant with falling leaves. A mourning dove on the branch above the window was saying goodbye to the day, between the swirling leaves and swaying of the limbs.

Ron, the agent, and I stood there, and I, with my back to them as they talked, remembered lighting the candle on that same windowsill that first night of the cafe. Their voices seemed to melt away, and vaguely aware they were in the same room with me, I was able, as if it was a heavenly gift, to call up the memory of that very first night of the cafe. It was so long ago, and yet for an instant, I summoned up that incredible heady anticipation of something really Big to come.

"Come on. I'll show you the upstairs." Said the agent.

I said those same words nine months before, in the darkness of the kitchen.

"They just gutted it too." She added, and headed up the stairs while Ron and I lagged behind.

"She keeps saying they *gutted* the place, but all they did was refinish the floors and put up different wallpaper. Oh, and two or three light fixtures." I whispered to Ron.

In the world of 'fixer uppers', a contractor had told me only a year before, my house was a Rehab Dream— there was hardly anything to do.

'They completely *redid* the bathroom."

"*Oh, no!*' I thought. "*Please don't say that. It was great, the blue and white wallpaper the white woodwork, the huge expanse of floor...*" I reached the top of the steps and looked inside. Nothing was different.

"It was originally a bedroom—" began the agent. I was mentally finishing her sentence. "but when they brought the plumbing indoors, they put the bathroom here..."

They had put on a new roof (the one that was on it when I bought the house was only six or seven years old, according to the former owners, but the valley where the ice tended to dam wasn't done properly). The chunk of fallen plaster was gone. One of the bedrooms was re-wallpapered, and the one that my other daughters had started to take the paper off of was untouched.

"They're going to be finishing the rest of the paper in the next month. Ready to see the outside?"

We walked downstairs and out the front door and around the side of the house toward the back.

"This is the original carriage house."

"Oh. Can we go inside?"

She seemed to hesitate. She didn't know that Maureen had once worked to make it a sort of tree-house. I had wanted to have it torn down, but with my job situation, it was really a matter of survival just to do the basics and the coffeehouse.

Once we came back down the steps, I mentioned I would probably have it torn down, that is, if it wasn't sound enough to restore.

As I reached the bottom step, I started to tell her that I had been the former owner, but I lost my footing on the edge of a fieldstone in the path at the bottom of the steps and it startled me. I didn't get a chance. What followed was incredible...

"I don't think the woman who lived here had it *even* a *YEAR*." began the agent. "She didn't do a *THING* to it! But the lady who lived here *before* that, well, SHE had *BEAU*tiful flowers. They were just *gorgeous*."

I thought of all the times total strangers came by and told me how pretty my flowers were. Usually, it was when I was outside working on the flower bed, but twice, passersby came up and *rang the bell* to tell me how much they enjoyed them. I always felt my flowers were a gift to other people.

I went numb. I couldn't believe what I was hearing.. I didn't know what to say. You always *think* you will know what to say when something like that happens, but when it does, all you can do is listen to them. Words fail you.

I glanced up at Ron and he caught my look but said nothing. We both let her go on and on. All I could do is stare at the back of the house, which I had scraped and sanded and primed the entire back wall in anticipation of being there long enough to repaint the house. Actually, some of the guys from The Open Door Cafe suggested we have a painting party and paint the house.

"The house was just a *WRECK*..." she continued. "What I mean is, it just didn't *show well*. Some of the walls were half-painted. Like

I said, the lady who lived here BEFORE had beautiful flowers all across the front of her house—— and SHE really kept it up."

"Well, you never know." I offered quietly. "Things happen."

I wanted to tell her that I was *both of those women*, and that during the year she was talking about, no one had even lived in the house. I had the car accident when I *would* have put in my flowers, (Mother's Day), and then we moved only three weeks later. Not only that, but the Main Street reconstruction project had started and the city had arranged an easement of my entire front yard for the project. They would have dug up all the flowers with backhoes anyway, so I gave them to Maureen just before we moved away.

We walked up the path which I had trimmed so many times— and part of it which I laid myself one early spring four years before. Continuing around to the front, she kept going on about "the former owner". Then as we stood on the front sidewalk, she pointed to the house across the street, where Gary and Marianne, my angels that one Christmas, had lived. "That house just sold a short time ago."

"It did? I don't go down this street very often." I offered. It was really hard to drive down my old street at all, so I usually found an alternative route.

I asked if Ron and I could step inside one more time.

Once inside, I pulled Ron's sleeve and we went into the living room.

Okay, I *dragged* him into the living room.

"Can you *believe* that?!"

He was smiling and tried to calm me down. He was terribly understanding. And terribly right.

"They *haven't* gutted it. Why is she *saying* that? I know exactly what they've done to it and what they haven't done! I should tell her who I am, that I lived here— and great things, really... *good* things— happened right here in these rooms!"

"I know." assured Ron. He *meant* that what the house *now was* was not important— and that somehow, we were given this last chance to say goodbye, for something greater lay beyond this.

We stood there and we prayed for the next part of The Plan to be revealed, for we didn't know what direction it would all take. We had felt like that Baker Street duo, Holmes and Watson, trying like all get-out to put together a puzzle that would solve the mystery.

Even now, as I write this, I don't yet know what the purpose of all of this was. Why did I have to love it so, and why did I have to lose it as well? To prove some spiritual principal— that we shouldn't get too attached to things here on earth?

I don't think so. Looking back on my life, I clearly see that all the times that I was frustrated about something, when I did something about it, the fruit of it was much bigger, on a much larger scale – than the initial frustrated plan. I wanted to learn to play the guitar. I never got one from my parents, though my brother did. But out of frustration, I learned to play Irish music on the hammered dulcimer, bodhran (a type of Irish drum), tin whistle and harmonica. When I had no place to go on Saturday night without placing myself in a vulnerable position where my testimony was concerned, I started The Open Door Cafe. I now see this pattern throughout my life, like a thread woven in fabric. It appears again and again.

So, then, out of my frustration at not *currently* being able to host a coffee house, I'm making darn sure, *by writing this book*, that at least a bunch of *other* people get to have a coffee house. The end result is that I always make the outcome much bigger than the initial desire!

This book has tremendous potential to change the way people approach loneliness and isolation, by empowering them to do something about it, and it completely blows out of the water all those statistics singles have read about. You know, where it's statistically more likely to be hit by a falling piano than it is that you'll marry after forty? This book, and the Open Door Cafe— prove all of that to be blarney, or malarkey. Whatever you want to call it. It will change the way you see your community, and the world you live in.

Ron went outside, and I stood alone in the house that was mine and then someone else's, where I could almost hear the faint tinkling of glasses, occasional laughter and distant strains of Irish fiddles and tin whistles from the rooms about me. I walked quietly from the living room, through the French doors and into the hallway. I sighed heavily, down into my soul, and stood by the front door. I turned around slowly, and looked through the hallway into the dining room to the back door, and, perhaps more importantly, *beyond*.

I reached up and turned off the hall light. Everything was dark once more and I smiled. I turned to open the screen door that I had opened to so many, and it was just heaven to simply open the door once more—and stepped out onto the front porch.

October was in full color. The bully winds that tumbled the leaves across the street and chased a newspaper through the small front yard brought a decided chill with it and recalled those first days of promise.

Ron was waiting on the sidewalk and the agent was on her phone in the driveway.

One last time, I closed the front door. The pain of losing most everything, made all my senses acute and keen. I was never more firmly convinced that forgiveness, grace, and most importantly love– were my fuel for making a difference, for waking the dead.. Reverently, prolonging the moment, listening for the comfort of the latch's click, I silently bid goodbye to The Open Door Cafe.

I had my children and the rest of my life. All of October lay before me.

"Well, " I said out loud, grinning. "— *anything* can happen. "It'll be fun! *You'll* see!"

APPENDIX

HOW TO SET UP AND RUN YOUR *OWN*

"OPEN DOOR CAFE"

"When's the last time you did something for the first time?"

I don't know who originated the above quote, but the first time I heard it, it stopped me in my tracks.

I realized that there are a great many people out there who haven't tried to do anything new in years. Maybe epochs. It is only a dim memory now. They don't remember what it was like those first exhilirating moments of realizing your bike was vertical —and you were *on* it. They have settled in to a routine that is safe, predictable and perfectly boring.

But Great Ideas are all around you. They are like diamonds waiting to be picked up. The trouble is, a lot of people have stopped looking down. They think they are not allowed to, like they're in some Diamond National Park and picking up of diamonds is not allowed. Of course, there are no signs that say "DIAMOND PICKING PROHIBITED". They just *think* there are, that perhaps they overlooked the signs, for they must be there somewhere—and that mindset alone prohibits them. Other people think that the diamonds will vanish in their grasp anyway, so what's the use? They just keep walking on that trail, ignoring the diamonds and wishing for a miracle. They may as well be walking down Madison Avenue or the isles of a grocery store, or the aisle of a church on Sunday morning.

Meanwhile, the diamonds, which would leap into the hands of the passersby if they possessed the power, go begging. "I'm down here! Can't you see me?" they call stonily.

I had always tried to live by the Life-Practice of Swashbuckling High Adventure, of looking for ways to accomplish something really big, and then going about the doing of it. Often in conceiving an idea (actually, of *uncovering* an idea, for it always seems to be there *already,* just waiting to be discovered), assembling the needed components (they are often there as well), and then letting it fly of its own accord.

Because of my own fascination with how this seems to take place, I find myself sharing this phenomena with all kinds of people. Usually *they* initiate the conversation, at first somewhat timidly, as if they anticipate a less than receptive reaction. They have been mugged by the people who don't believe in the miraculous.

This is because in our world and with our hectic lifestyle, we are seldom quiet enough or alert enough when we are at last in solitude, to get a big idea to begin with— much less recognize a *miracle* when we see one. (to those who *disbelieve*, I say, "Don't worry. If you don't believe in miracles, then you won't have any."). When we are in the solitude of our own company, that's when we'll switch on the radio or the TV or call a friend. The quiet is uncomfortable and reminds us of our ultimate isolation. It is scary.

The Miracle Makers, however, will use words such as, "Calling" or "I don't know why, but..." Then they will proceed to share with you, almost tearfully, the thing they feel some compelling urge to do or accomplish. Often they don't know why it is that they feel compelled to do so. They are not talking irrationally, and it is not a delusion.

They are being prompted by God to do something and it is invariably for the good of many, not just the person who has the dream of doing something. The trouble is, they have been beset by Bubble Busters who don't really get it. In fact, Bubble Busters and Dream Dusters seem to stand in line, waiting for a whack at diverting, dismantling and destroying someone else's idea. Moreover, the would be Miracle Makers have had to overcome plenty of their own self-inflicted Bubble Busting tendencies to even conceive the idea in the first place. With the pain of doubt and cynicism fresh in their minds, and knowing full well the objections— and eyebrows— that will be raised by others (because they themselves raised them), they are gun-shy when it comes to exposing their dreams to the scrutiny of careless observers and disinterested bystanders.

Against all odds, despite all nay-sayers, they must persevere, because a very Great Deal is at stake.

The book you are reading is the result of a Great Adventure. The adventure happened in the pursuit of a really good cup of coffee, but ended in true romance. It will instruct you in the startup and operation of what I believe will become a national trend, the home-based coffeehouse. Although it concerns coffee, it really concerns a whole lot more and serves as a model for *other types* of Miracle Making.

And your realization of a dream come true is only one of the perks.

DEFINING YOUR CAFE AND YOUR PURPOSE

What in the world *is* a Home Cafe, anyhow?

A loose definition is:

"A gathering of people, usually of similar circumstances, at a home or home-like environment, for the purpose of lively conversation, fellowship, sharing of common life-experiences and the making of new friends on a deep and satisfying level."

I made the above definition up just now, but I *lived* it for four years.

I am a single mother of five, and I had a quaint pink, purple and turquoise Victorian house located in a small town north of Cincinnati, Ohio. I was also the Singles Ministry leader for my church. Because I love traditional Irish music, jazz, and the blues, I longed for a place to go on a given night of the week where I wouldn't feel that I had to compromise my Christian lifestyle, a place dedicated to Christian Singles. Where the people I would meet would, for the most part, share my values.

I certainly didn't have any money to buy or rent any real estate. But **instead of dismissing the idea** entirely, I fantasized about what it would look like. I decided it would be really great if it looked like my home. It was furnished in antiques, had charming wallpaper and architectural features, and a wonderfully cozy atmosphere.

Then a weird thought came to me. *"What if I hosted a coffee house in my house?"* I was already doing a coffee house at my church, but with a new construction project in the works, I lost the room that I was using. Immediately, my imagination took off, and I developed the Home Cafe concept from there. It was called "The Open Door Cafe", and you can read the whole story behind the cafe as well as a sampling of what *really* went on behind Open Doors, in my book, Saturday Night at The Open Door Cafe. In the four short years I operated the cafe, twenty people met their mate at my house, and it was featured nationally in *Today's Christian Woman Magazine.*

The rest is really history, and I'll be sharing some it with you throughout the course of this book.

The Home Cafe is a meeting of people who are, initially, total strangers. Oh, there may be a few people who know each other, but basically the door is always, well, open. Although you may not know anyone from Adam, eventually everyone gets to know one another and deep and lasting friendships develop. I can't imagine not knowing some of the people who came to my home.

The format of your Home Cafe is as unique as you are, and as interesting as your guests. All you have to do is learn the basics of what to do and what not to do, and you'll be the host of your own night spot.

I know right now some of you are cringing. You have a lot of questions, and they are perfectly valid. As you read on, I'll address some key aspects that will make your Home Cafe absolutely safe, immensely enjoyable, and richly rewarding for you and your guests.

The first question you want to ask yourself is why you want to host a Home Cafe in the first place. Why would anyone go to the trouble of inviting a bunch of complete strangers into their home, serving desserts, hors d'oeuvres, and great coffee?

Because in our society, loneliness and the resulting depression have devastating consequences on people's emotional well-being.

There is a genuine need for people of all ages and walks of life to find camaraderie and fellowship. The trouble is, the opportunities for this kind of interaction are few. A lot of people have no where to go to find the rewarding relationships I'm speaking of. Most churches, in fact, don't offer small group meetings to encourage the knowing of one another. It's one of humanity's greatest needs, that of being understood and known by their fellow man. We were, after all, created to be in relationship to one another.

The reasons for such widespread loneliness and isolation are many. Some are situational in nature, such as the young single man who works third shift and is on a completely different sleep schedule than other people his own age. For others, loneliness is the result of simply having no opportunities to interact on a deeper level.

People travel for their jobs and lose touch with those who mean the most to them. Often they find themselves in a strange town or city, and aside from co-workers, have very little opportunity for interaction. They live in a subdivision and perhaps because they have moved so often they are reluctant to build new friendships. Think about it. How many of your own neighbors do *you* know?

In the case of college and career-age young people, who are commonly facing some issues of independence as they leave home; but struggling to get careers started and making new friends on a campus away from home are daunting, especially for people who are shy to begin with. They can profit from the knowledge that their comrades are pretty much in the same boat— and they can likewise benefit from sharing strategies with one another.

Singles, a *huge* group who often find themselves dating again after a divorce or death of their partner, generally have no place to gather with other singles, except in a bar setting. Rather than face that prospect— after all, where are you gonna go?— they resort to going home to a barren apartment. Time after time, I've heard, "Where can you go to meet some nice people? If I go to a bar, it's pretty likely I'll meet someone who hangs out at a bar." I always want to answer, "Well, maybe you could meet them at your house..."

Seniors are another large group which could greatly benefit from a home cafe. Like the college and career age folk, their needs are common. They are all dealing with lifestyle changes, the desire for wellness in every aspect of their life, and some of them have already lost close friends and family. They especially appreciate the warmth of solid friendships. The seniors of today are actually more and more active later into their lives than in the past, some of them are even starting businesses just when they thought they wanted to retire. They are looking for travelling companions, golfing companions, bridge partners and any number of interest-sharing compatriots.

You probably already know that there is extensive documentation that people just plain live longer when they enjoy regular interaction and fellowship with a bunch of others— *and*, it improves the *quality* of their life.

Are you beginning to see the possibilities? The combinations and focus are unlimited— with a little imagination.

You see, a whole bunch of people are sitting at home and they are just plain lonely. They don't talk about it, because for some reason they don't want to admit it. After all, if we *really* have our act together, why would we be lonely in the first place? That is a Really Big Myth. They've been looking at their problem of loneliness all backwards. If you don't have a place to go, make one yourself. If no one you know invites people over, then you invite *them*. If you don't know anyone, well, there's a solution for that as well. There just aren't any excuses any more to be lonely with nothing to do and no place to go. Your life is getting ready to change for the better— along with a whole lot of other people..

You may be thinking "But... I can't......"

Stop that! If I could do it so can you— or anybody. You just need some more information on how to go about it. The hardest objections we ever have to overcome are often our own. Or maybe your job is to pass this information on to someone. I would be willing to bet you know someone with a knack for entertaining or cooking of who just likes to nurture and spoil people.

Believe me, that's all it takes.

A word of caution, here though, and I'm very serious about this. What you are undertaking when you start up a Home Cafe is a great and noble thing that meets an important need in your community.

It is *never* going to be All About You.

You may be stellar at entertaining. You may be flamboyant and extravagant, and you may have a lovely home lavishly appointed. Hosting a Home Cafe is not about the spotlight being aimed in your direction or at your accomplishments in decorating. If it were, you would be missing one of the greatest rewards, that of receding into the background and watching the Miraculous happen. You would enjoy the center of the stage for a time, but in the end, it would somehow seem a little flat. Just as in the saying "it is more blessed to give than to receive", there is a certain depth of appreciation and receiving that comes as a result of the giving. Mother Theresa is not remembered because she thought greatly of herself or even little of herself, but in that *she didn't really think of herself at all.* Yet, look at the tremendous good she did among many.

On the other hand, perhaps you *don't* have the perfect house (who really *does*?) and perhaps your furnishings are gently worn and even a little shabby. This too, is shining the spotlight on you. Some of the best times I've ever had are conversations unblushingly honest, shared over a mutual peanut butter sandwich and Celestial Seasonings Mandarin Orange Spice tea. No one ever seemed to mind the little wobble of a chair, or the chip in a saucer at my house.

So, the *why* is to be found in a Greater Purpose, something that extends beyond you and the few you know, to a vast circle of *friends yet-to-be*, of good heartedness and self- sacrifice. And yes, someone may drop a fork or spill their coffee. But most little accidents are easily tidied up amid laughter and apologies while eating Humble Pie.

How wonderfully human it all is.

SETTING

The next thing to consider upon the decision to host a Home Cafe is what makes the best setting. There are some important considerations in determining a location, and some of them may rule out that particular place. Not to worry, though, because there are usually some very good alternatives available.

I should mention here that it is not a good idea to invest in any real estate. There are good reasons for this. If you only meet one or even two nights a week, not to mention once a month, the place is sitting empty. If you allow someone else the use of it, they must be trustworthy and respect your wishes with regard to off-limit areas, etc. There are times when this could work, for example if it is a ministry and you have a not-for-profit organization that serves as an umbrella. But this gets into a legal sticky wicket and involves more of a full-time operation.

For university students, ask about using a room in the Student Union. There may be a deposit, so please make sure you are a good citizen and you will get your deposit back. Some dorms have lounge facilities, so you may reserve one. There are also likely places on or around campus, some with really unique interiors and architectural features, which make a cozy meeting spot. Perhaps one of the professors or a neighborhood pastor would be interested in serving as a host if for no other reason than to keep their finger on the pulse of youthful thinking.

Career-age people, twenties or early thirties, may find it's pretty easy to meet at a local restaurant that has a meeting room. Just call ahead and arrange to reserve the room. Have some signage to indicate where you are meeting. Whenever you decide to meet at a restaurant, call ahead to tell them that a group is coming. It's considerate and expected. Also, leave a generous tip for the person who is waiting on you.

If you are hosting the cafe at your home, it is a very good idea if you can host the cafe on a single floor with no steps to climb to the restroom. This way, it is easier to deter peoples' access to areas you want to maintain as private.

My bedroom in my Victorian house was made out of a first-floor study and it had a fireplace in it. My daughter's bedrooms were upstairs, as I had four daughters still at home at the time (there were only two bedrooms—there had been a third originally, but when they moved the plumbing inside, they used a bedroom for the bathroom). I decided that if I took down my four poster bed and slept on my loveseat, I would have the entire downstairs available to hostess the coffee house in. I have to say that I didn't mind sleeping on my loveseat (I used to be a lot taller though— just kidding... actually, I've *always* been five feet tall) because *the vision of doing something on a scale like this was so-oo-oo much more captivating than my temporary comfort.*

To my way of thinking, lots of missionaries sleep on the floor of a hut— or a jail cell for that matter— for their ministry. It seemed the least I could do. The trade-off was being able to do something that was tons of fun.

What follows are some aspects for consideration in making your decision on the location of your Home Cafe.

ENTRANCES AND EXITS

One important thing would be accessibility, particularly if you have anyone elderly or impaired who will be attending. You certainly don't want to exclude anyone based on their inability to negotiate steps. Even college and career- aged patrons occasionally break a leg playing football or soccer. This doesn't mean that you have to have ramps built onto the front of your house either. You just don't want to live on the second or third floor of an apartment and ask all those people to climb umpteen steps. Ideally, a short flight of steps from a front or rear walkway is good. Hilly terrain might make things difficult, so having an alternate entry for your guests will make everyone feel that they have access. Sometimes people come in wheelchairs, too, the result of a car accident or home remodeling project gone terribly awry. Plan for the general public where you can.

SAFETY

Keep entryways clear of signage, clutter or decorative items that could be knocked over or tripped over. At Christmas time, make certain there are no wild extension cords creeping across walkways or porches. Also, make certain your walkway and porch are well lit, turning on the porch light before it even becomes dark. Sometimes on a busy night, it becomes dark before you know it while you were engaged in a lively discussion.

Another issue of great importance is Fire Safety, especially if you plan to burn candles, incense or you have a fireplace. Some sites I looked at were above shops in my small town. The town itself has a lot of antique shops and the buildings are old. The spaces above the shops are apartments and such, with loo-oo-nnngg flight of steps to them. They are unusable as cafe space because of the risk of entrapment if there was a fire or other emergency. This was despite the fact that they had charming garrets and beams and brickwork. You will want to have two or more exits if you can. Of course, there may be local restrictions as to the number of occupants, so if your group gets to be of any appreciable size, please inquire from your local fire department and follow exactly any instructions they give you. Make certain you have properly installed smoke alarms and that they are in good working order. Test them regularly, and make a note on your calendar when you are to replace the batteries. It is a good idea to have a fire escape plan drawn with the exits indicated and in an area most everyone will see, such as the back of the bathroom door.

Since we're talking about candles and such, let me stress how important it is for candles to be in safe places where they are unlikely to be knocked over, or bumped into— on a mantle or in an enclosed decorative holder, on a buffet or other suitable place. Yes, they look cool in other places, like going up the stairs for example, but you are asking for singed clothing or injury. Don't do it. It isn't worth the risk of injury.

RESTROOMS

The location of restrooms is important, once again, for accessibility. In an ideal world, there would be a half bath on the first floor in a less than central location.

You will need to decide if you wish your guests to go upstairs. When I ran my Home Cafe, the upstairs was completely off-limits. I had four daughters at home at the time and the upstairs was their space. After all, I was having a bunch of Old People" in our home every week and they needed to be able to have their privacy too.

You needn't have assist grips or anything because you are not a business. The door should, however, have a lock on it. If there isn't one, then you need to put one on it. A lot of people, for whatever reason, assume that a closed bathroom door doesn't necessarily mean no one is using it, and so will attempt to open the door, even if they see the light is shining beneath it. Inexpensive locks are available, so you don't have to put on a whole new door.

It is important that the bathroom's location be somewhat *away* from the general flow of guests. This is for rather obvious reasons, but I'll go ahead and address it here. You want to extend to your guests using the restroom a degree of privacy and discretion, considering their modesty. In addition, you want to preserve the gracious atmosphere *outside* the bathroom door, lest your guests be embarrassed. Therefore, you either need to have a bathroom in a somewhat removed location, or perhaps locate the stereo speakers in close proximity to the bathroom/gathering area.

I will discuss how the bathroom might be appointed later.

PARKING

The best scenario is to have on street parking, making sure none of your guests block fire hydrants. If you live across the street from a church or nine-to-five business, ask if it would be all right if your guests use their lot after hours. In appreciation, you may want to extend an open door invitation to the employees or church members, and occasionally drop off a small gift, a plate of cookies or a box of chocolates.

Discourage your guests from parking in your neighbors' spots. Masking tape an x if you have a particularly fussy neighbor.

If you live in an apartment or condo complex or even a retirement community, you may only be allotted a spot for your personal car. If so, ask if you may use the complex clubhouse. They may charge a small refundable deposit of, say, $25. Always be sure to clean and tidy any area you use.

If you have a spacious back yard with a driveway, you may want to have some additional pavement, such as gravel or even a truckload of mulch extending your park-able space. If space to park is limited you can encourage guests to come in groups, or shuttle from a nearby shopping center lot. If there is *no* parking, then you may want to locate the cafe elsewhere.

YOUR NEIGHBORHOOD

What if your house is okay but you aren't in the best of neighborhoods? You may want to consider relocating to a friend's neighborhood where the general environment generates a safer feel. Or, contact your local police department via their non-emergency line. Tell them that you are hosting a gathering on a regular basis and communicate your concerns. The intention of your gathering is a positive one and probably welcome in the community. Invite them to stop by and greet your guests or drive by to indicate their presence. Solicit help from area churches to help you promote your Home Cafe.

Some neighborhoods have associations that you must check with and sometimes you may find that they aren't really in favor of your idea. Sometimes this is just orneriness, but other times it is because the streets are too narrow to permit parking on the street *and* allow access by emergency vehicles.

ON BEING A GOOD NEIGHBOR

In hosting a Home Cafe, you automatically become a Presence in the community. People always wonder why there are all those cars parked in front of your house, the music, and the laughter— all those trays of cookies... What are you waiting for? Invite them too!

Having a presence in your neighborhood can, however, be a little unsettling or even intimidating for some of your neighbors. Perhaps they will feel excluded. They may feel invaded or as if their tranquility is being disturbed. They, for whatever reason, are just annoyed that someone is having fun.

This is the time to be extra gracious, extra kind, maybe mowing their grass once in a while or offering to pick something up for them while you are running errands. Sometimes just a small note of appreciation can be left with a pot of tulips on their porch, just for them being a good sport about it all.

The Home Cafe is not about showing off, but about showing *up*. Initiate contact. Explain to your neighbors what you are going to be doing on Friday or Saturday nights— perhaps Sunday afternoons— along with a sincere invitation to join you. You are automatically going to be a sort of liaison and hub of information. Many of them may become your favorite guests, even if things start off rocky at first.

Okay, so now imagine your Home Cafe in a location which is safe, well-lit and charming. There may even be more than one cafe in a given neighborhood. That's okay too. It isn't about competition (remember the spotlight?) it's about communication. Their cafe may be different than yours. Great. What some people like about your Home Cafe may be different than what others like about theirs. Diversity is always good because it keeps things from being boring. Some of your guests may attend two or three cafes (imagine that!) just to keep things interesting.

The actual numbers of attendees are no indication of success, either. Just because a lot of people come to a particular Home Cafe doesn't mean any deep sharing is going on. Remember, it is often easier to be anonymous in a crowd than in a small group.

I once had thirty-eight people at my house. I had five downstairs rooms and a deck for them to use. It was nice, but really too noisy to hear and therefore put it on the level of sincerity of a dance or a bar. The most intimate and poignant conversations occurred when there were only a handful of guests per room, and occasionally when there were only three to five people left at the end of and evening. Your guests are much more likely to open up and take off the mask when there are only a few of them. That is where real brotherhood and sisterhood happen.

Never allow yourself to become competitive or jealous. If you notice those feelings creeping in, then you are off the track and your attitude has become one of showing off. You may need to pray to overcome those feelings, especially if you began the Home Cafe in your neighborhood and someone else sees it as a competition. Congratulate yourself on having gotten the ball rolling (perhaps that was the divine plan to begin with) and relax at the other person's cafe.

The main idea is that it got started and now you can bless everybody's socks off!

MEETING TIMES

Where you host your Home Cafe is really flexible and adds to the fun. Moreover, *when* you host the cafe and the *consistency* will help or hinder your attendance.

You want to meet on a regular basis. That way, people will not forget when the meeting is. Consistency insures a feeling of continuity. One group I know has First Friday Parties. The hosting home is always different, and to let everyone know the details, they make a flyer and hand it out to their neighbors. Then they make a tray of hors d'ouevres and bring a beverage.

Saying the first Saturday of the month or the last Friday is okay. The only trouble with monthly meetings is that it takes longer for everyone to get to know each other. If you trade off among four houses or more, then the burden (if it presents a challenge it's a burden—if you love entertaining, you may think it takes forever to be 'your turn') won't be on just one person.

When I did my singles ministry, we started off meeting every final Saturday. One of the guys commented, "You know Caron, I *love* this! The only trouble is, I'm single all month!" It took a long time for me to commit to an every week thing. First of all, we initially met in a classroom at the church. By day it was a toddler classroom, but on the final Saturday of the month, it became a... *living room*, complete with drapes, pictures (instead of bulletin boards and Noah's animals), occasional tables lamps, wing chairs and espresso machine. It was an all day endeavor, transforming and schlepping (a nice Yiddish word for draggin' a bunch of stuff everywhere)— and then at six the next morning I had to transform it all back so that the toddlers could use it.

Was I *nuts*?

I didn't want to commit to doing the cafe weekly because, well, I was a little selfish about my time. After all, I wanted to reserve MY weekends for times when I wanted to do something like, well, take a weekend trip or something. Not that I ever did. It was just that I wanted the freedom to "just in case". Once I realized that the just-in-cases weren't even happening, and the idea of having a party every weekend seemed more fun than anything I would have thought of to do on a weekend, the rest was easy.

There were times when I did have to go out of town, but I arranged to have trustworthy people host the cafe in my absence. I made sure all the ingredients were there or that they purchased ready made trays and cookies from the neighborhood grocery store. Then, they reimbursed themselves from the cafe kitty or tip jar, leaving the receipt inside the jar. It went off without hardly a hitch.

So you want to have it on a regular basis, hopefully once a week. There is an unseen benefit of doing this.

I cannot tell you how often I heard from the people who came to my house that they looked forward all week to coming to Caron's Open Door Cafe. It was the place where they got a hug, a pat on the back, a compliment, a kind word. They could dress up a little once they got the grass mowed and the groceries for the next week stocked up and count on an evening of talking on their level, and sharing on a deeper one..

Saturday nights there was something to look forward to.

No matter how difficult the week was, no matter how lonely, they could put on a little cologne, a little aftershave, bring a book they were reading to share or make their own fancy dessert, and head over to Caron's. Those poignant little cards and words of thanks made all of it worthwhile, and I will never forget them. I kept all the cards.

Fridays are good, but if people have had to work and don't get done commuting until a half hour before you start, then they are less likely to go back out. Often they will want to go home and change clothes as well as gears. Sometimes it's really hard to get the inspiration to go back out.

Saturdays worked well for me because it gave me all day to clean, polish, cook and otherwise prepare to treat my guests like royalty. It is so much easier to entertain when you've had a full day to prepare, and you feel more confident that there aren't water spots on the silverware. Not only that, but there were invariably little touches I would add that particular week to decorate. I always liked to change things around just a little. It was never the same coffeehouse two weeks in a row.

The time of your meeting day —or night— should allow people time to get home from soccer games with kids, the grocery store, finish their own house cleaning and otherwise prepare to visit.

The time frame should not be open-ended, otherwise people will stay all night. I had to kick people out at two in the morning sometimes so I could go to church the next day. I would jokingly say, "Okay, guys, just turn out the lights and lock the door when you leave." And head toward the stairs (even though I slept on my loveseat). "We feel so at home here we hate to leave!" they would say.

Therefore, a good block of time is, say, four hours. I always hosted the cafe from 7PM to 11PM. That's four hours. Often some people stayed later, but the point is, *there's always next time*. If they hate to leave, that's a pretty good indication that they'll be back next week. After all, you don't want to burn yourself out either. You'll always be fresh and prepared if you set limits. You never want to feel taken advantage of.

If you are the *guest* of a Home Cafe, please be considerate of your host or hostess. They have usually worked all week themselves, they have a family and they have commitments the next day. We'll address other House Rules later.

One young woman who attended my Home Cafe borrowed my idea and set up coffeehouses in three churches on three nights of the week/month. This is attributed to her marvelous organizational skills. She approached me at the wedding shower of one of the people who met their mate at my house, and said, "I don't know if you remember me, because I only came once. But I took your idea back with me and was able to put together a group of people who take turns hosting an Open Door Cafe of our own."

I did remember her, and though there were times that I thought the cafe had died with the final meeting, I was, at that moment, convinced of the far-reaching and lasting impact of all those Saturday nights.

PROMOTING AND FUNDING YOUR HOME CAFE

Promoting your cafe is actually pretty easy. Once people find out you're doing this, particularly in a retirement community or campus, you may find yourself scouting garage sales for extra chairs. I always seemed to have bunches of chairs, and I joked that i had more chairs than a Shaker meeting house.

Never pay for advertising because you can usually get all the people you need just by doing the free stuff. Your city or local newspaper usually has aa section geared toward community events, where you can advertise your home cafe. You might inquire if they can give it a heading, such as "Singles". My ad ran something like this:

The Open Door Cafe Christian Singles meets every 'single' Saturday night at 417 E. Main St., Lebanon, OH, 7 PM-11PM. Enjoy freshly-brewed gourmet coffee and delectable desserts while engaging in lively conversation with new friends. Suggested donation $3 helps with costs. For more information, call Caron at 555-5555.

If there is a community bulletin board at your neighborhood grocery store, then ask if you may post a flier. Make a flier with little 'tear-offs' so that people can pass it along to a friend. Make sure that there are no bloopers on your flier and that all the necessary information is there. Include abbreviated directions if your house is in a challenging location as well as details like "Parking in rear."

You might also post fliers in libraries, churches, schools and area shops.

Don't overlook community, school, church and organization newsletters. Editors are often looking for information about your very Home Cafe. And, telephone your local community paper for a possible write-up. Provide them with a brief description of your cafe, it's decor, your fare, and possibly yourself. Tell them what makes it unique. It makes a great human interest story.

There are various ways to fund your cafe, but the easiest way is directly by donations of the attendees.

The Home Cafe is *not* a business. You must not confuse it with a coffee "shop". If you make a profit at this, then you are doing it for all the wrong reasons and you must declare it as income, and register with your state and Federal Government so you can pay taxes on your earnings. It is donation based, and the cost is small. I *suggested* a donation of $3. This usually covered the cost of the food, coffee, soda and lemonade, etc. Many times it did not, because I love to cook and made rather elaborate dishes. If you *charge* rather than *suggest,* you place your gathering into a whole different tax category and you must meet local and state Board of Health Regulations and Codes.

If you consider your Home Cafe to be a ministry, then you may want to contact area pastors and explain your concept to them. If it is an interfaith mainstream Christian coffeehouse, then they may want to help you offset some of the costs so that you don't need to charge any donation at all.

In deciding what to suggest, keep it well within the budgets of your attendees. I never wanted $3 to come between a single mom or dad or anyone else for that matter, and making friends. If they missed one week, they usually 'caught up' the next.

You should have a small guest book in a prominent place near the front door. Ask people to sign in if they haven't been there before, and that way you can send them a newsletter or notify them of changes and special events. I like to know people's birthdays and extra stuff so I can send them a card. In your guest book, you will probably want space for comments or to communicate prayer needs.

Next to your guest book keep the 'Kitty" or tip jar. This is where people will put their donations. Make it clear, such as a cut glass or crystal bowl. That way people can remember to contribute and also they can make change. I never really worried about how much was——or wasn't—in the tip jar, because I did it for the love of the people who came to my house and placed a little faith in me. It always seemed to work out just fine.

A couple of times, people donated a sizeable sum to the cafe. I used it to purchase a loveseat for additional seating and a new stereo (the one I was using would always get stuck on the CD and someone would say, "It's stuck again, Caron" so I would always have to baby-sit the CD player).

Your integrity is crucial. Your guests have placed a certain degree of trust in you, in the belief that you are doing this out of a love for serving others. You must never ever betray the confidence they have placed in you. You must always use Home Cafe funds for Home Cafe business. Anything else smacks of opportunism and kinda gives me the willies. It becomes self focused and for one's own gain, which is *so* "not the purpose". If the cafe has no immediate needs, consider whether one of your guests has a need in their life, or if you might make a charitable donation in the Home Cafe's name.

WHAT TO SERVE

Now that you have a lot of the logistics out of the way, you can concentrate on the fare of your Home Cafe. To some of you, this is the best part. Others of you are cringing. Not to worry, because even if you are a terrible cook, you can still host a great Home Cafe.

For the cuisine challenged, there are plenty of options that will get you out of the cooking aspect. You can purchase easy to make desserts which require little expertise. My ten year old was making a lot of the food I served at the cafe and loves to cook to this day. In addition, you can purchase lots of restaurant grade desserts from places like Sam's Club, Costco, or Gordon Foodservice (Gordon is open to the public with no membership fees).

Another option is to offer your guests the option of bringing a pot luck dessert in lieu of contributing to the Coffee House Kitty. This gives your guest the opportunity to showcase their interest in cooking and makes everyone feel special who is on the sampling end of it.

The point is, just because you are the host doesn't mean that you are necessarily doing all the cooking. Keep it rather simple in the beginning, until you get your "sea legs". Once you establish a method of operation, you can then do more challenging things.

What follows is a cornucopia of tips and suggestions that will alleviate some of your concerns with entertaining the general public.

- Always introduce your guests. Meet them at the door if you are free to do so and ask them a little about themselves. Then, relate this information as you introduce them. Give them the nickel tour of the area that is open to the cafe, and show them where the restroom is. Have them sign the guest book with name address and phone, as well as an email address, if they have one.
- Often, people will ask if they can help with anything (usually because they are nervous), so if you can, allow them to assist with putting trays of cookies out or something.
- Have some games available, but don't stress the playing of them. A lot of times people will have a hard time making connections and talking if the games prove to be distracting.
- Music should be loud enough to fill in the blanks, but not loud enough to be a distraction. Non vocal is usually a good choice, because lyrics, particularly well known lyrics can be intrusive. After all, you want your guests to get to know one another. Jazz, classical, Celtic, Renaissance— all are good choices. Never choose something vulgar or questionable.
- Keep a stockpile of easy things to serve that can be made in a jiffy— just in case you get a few more guests than usual.
- Your fare is not limited to desserts only. Besides, some of your guests may have health concerns, like diabetes. Try to anticipate a lot of the needs so that everyone can graze on something.
- Always try to vary what you are serving, including hot and cold, sweet and not sweet, Decaf and regular. This keeps things interesting.
- Once you have made the initial investment, you will mainly be replenishing your stock of dessert mixes, beverages, etc.
- I always went to the grocery store on Saturday morning so that the fruit and veggies were as fresh as I could get.
- I started the food preparations at 3PM and the cafe began at 7PM. That gave me four hours to garnish, fuss, brew, and correct cooking blunders before anyone would arrive.

- Make certain you have all the napkins and silverware you will need. Keep plastic tableware in case you run out of silverware.
- Pick up extra cups and saucers at your neighborhood Goodwill or thrift store. There are often pretty pieces and it doesn't really matter if things don't match.
- I used a West Bend coffee maker (the 55 cup size) after several others (one was an expensive model that only lasted three months) wore out or proved to be too small. Air pots are okay, but you still find yourself brewing coffee throughout the night unless you have a lot of air pots. They are often just an added expense. Unless you have the good ones that are around $50-60 they don't keep the coffee as hot and they don't hold as much.
- Serve everything buffet style. If you have a kitchen counter that will work good, but you can also use a dining room table, a sideboard or buffet or an antique piece that will work. Protect the surface!
- In protecting the surface, you can use plastic table cloths, place mats, silver trays (these worked well for me) table runners, or china.
- If you can, stack your cups and saucers on one another, cup saucer, cup saucer, etc. Sometimes the cups will fit right into the bottom of the saucer above it. Don't stack too high though. This will save room. You can also have a BIG mug rack and allow everyone to choose their favorite. Again, your local thrift shop always has bunches of mugs and they're inexpensive.
- Keep it together. Have one area for beverages and another for food if you can. Where the coffee is, so should be the cream or creamer, sugar and sugar substitutes, stir sticks, a waste can (for stir sticks and napkins etc.) teas and flavoring syrups.
- Feel free to use things for what they were never intended. I used an armoire/entertainment unit to keep the coffee urn, cups saucers, and all the supplies in. I lined the back of it with lovely dramatic fabric, placed white Christmas lights all around the opening and toward the back of the shelves and when Saturday night was over I just closed up the whole shootin' match until the next Saturday. Use baskets for serving pieces, teapots for fresh flowers, candles instead of a real fire in a fireplace, a hall table turned diagonally in the foyer as a maitre d' station (for the guest books and kitty), watering cans,

tool boxes, YOU NAME IT. Use your imagination to turn everyday objects into part of the cafe. Create themes. I brought corn shocks and mums and pumpkins inside for a fall display in a corner of the dining room. Then, I used two antique windows hinges together like shutters to frame a poinsettia display at Christmas time. Change things around to go with seasons or holidays.

- If you lack giftedness in any of these areas, then work as a team with guests who do have talent with cooking and decorating, and make it a collaborative effort. No one person always possesses *all* the ability. Don't feel threatened by someone else's abilities. *When you are truly unique, you don't have competition.* Soliciting help from others helps them feel needed and helps you develop bonds of interdependence. Think of it as training proteges.
- In the bathroom you will want to have adequate guest towels. You can put paper towels there if you like, or purchase paper guest towels(this gets expensive long term, however). Decorate the bathroom to, for seasons and holidays. Keep air freshener nearby and you might also place a fancy dish of mints on the vanity.
- The bathroom is a good place to post a list of "House Rules" too. Believe it or not, some people will stay all night, go through drawers looking for a pen, and look through kitchen cabinets for something a little more spicy for the hors d'ouevres. This way, you can communicate your expectations about behavior, without having to spell it out verbally. Placing it in the bathroom allows people to read it privately and since it's likely that most people will use the bathroom on occasion, you can make sure everyone is on the same page.

THERE YOU HAVE IT!

This has been the nutshell version of the do-it-yourself Home Cafe. By following the guidelines I've given you, you should be able to have a cafe experience without hocking the house and kids. You won't need a business degree, restaurant experience, a bank loan, or real estate.

What you will get is the cafe of your dreams because it's all you! You will provide a much needed service to your community and town, and all because you chose to think outside of the general perimeters of the rhombus (box).

You *can* do this, you know and you will be amply rewarded by the cards you will inevitably get (sometimes anonymously) and the friends you will make in the process. Nothing will prepare you for the wonderful and rewarding experience you will have in hosting your own Home Cafe.

MORE QUESTIONS?

If you would like more information or you have some logistic problems, please feel free to contact me at caron222@netzero.com. and please enter Open Door Cafe in the subject line. I would love to help you! Look for the companion book, *Secrets of The Open Door Cafe* coming soon. It will offer valuable information on how to host a cafe in *your* home (or off-site).

Printed in the United States
128062LV00002B/36/A